MARYLEBONE
& TYBURN PAST

Acknowledgements

We wish to thank the following for their help and support in the writing of this book. Richard Bowden, Archivist of the Portman and Howard de Walden Estates; the John Lewis Archive, Stevenage; Selfridges Archive; Janice Liversege, Royal Society of Medicine; Mark Riddaway, editor *Marylebone Journal*; the staff of the Guildhall Library, London and the City of Westminster Archives; Oliver Bradbury; Ann Saunders; Helen English for her proof reading and constructive suggestions and John Richardson for his advice and help with the illustrations.

First published 2007
by Historical Publications Ltd
32 Ellington Street, London N7 8PL
(Tel: 020 7607 1628)

ISBN 978-1-905286-17-1
British Library Cataloguing-in-Publication Data
A catalogue record for this book is available from the British Library

Typeset by Historical Publications Ltd
Reproduction by Tintern Graphics
Printed in Zaragoza, Spain by Edelvives

The Illustrations

The following have kindly given permission to produce illustrations:
John Lewis Archive *94, 95*
London Topographical Society, *frontispiece and 78*
Meschino family archive, Magadino *79*
Paul Rothe *47*
St Marylebone Society *2, 4, 111*
Westminster City Archives *59, 102, 103, 112*
Wigmore Hall *121*

The Authors *19, 30, 65, 66, 72, 76, 128*
Other illustrations were supplied by the Publisher.

MARYLEBONE & TYBURN PAST

David Brandon
Alan Brooke

HISTORICAL PUBLICATIONS

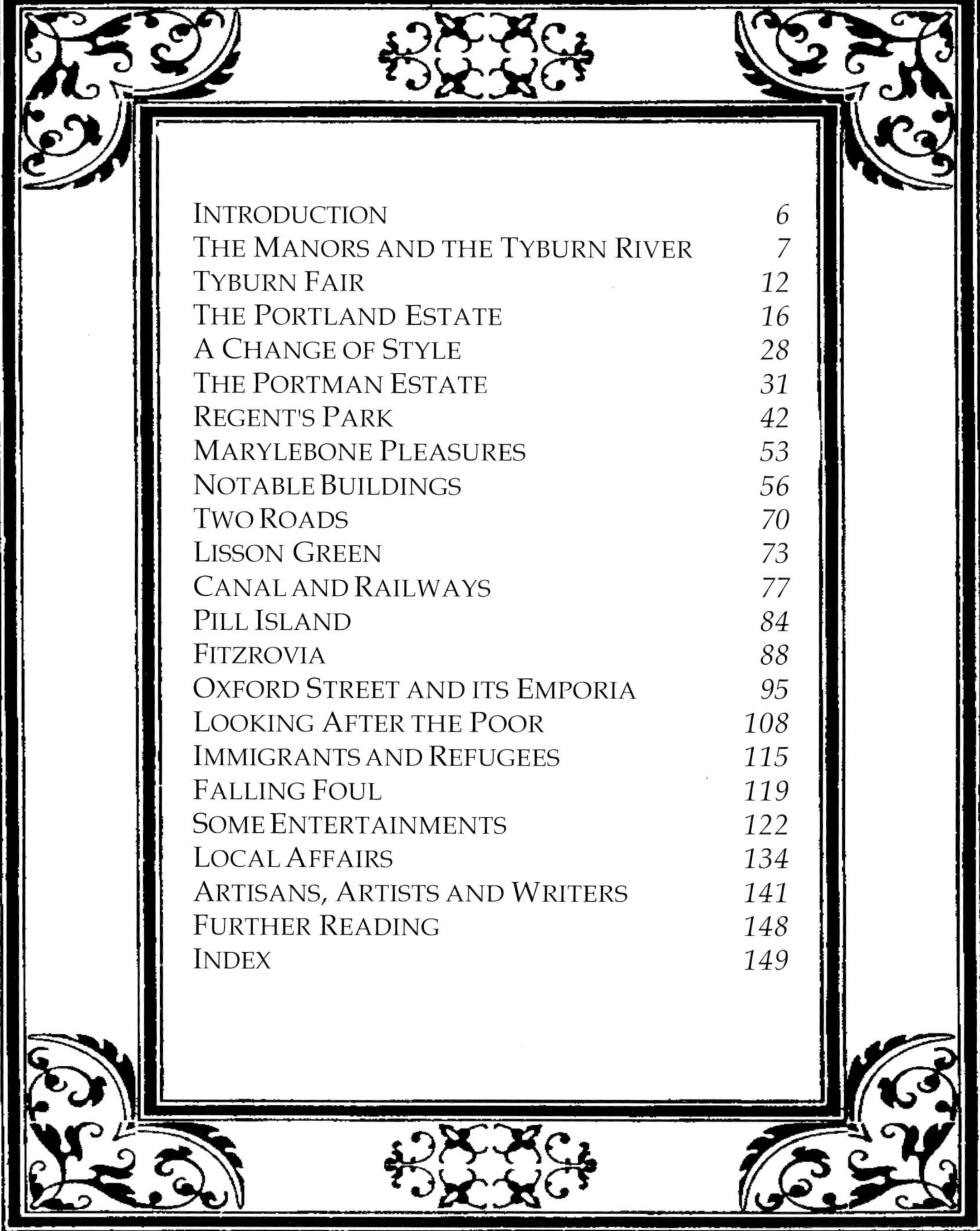

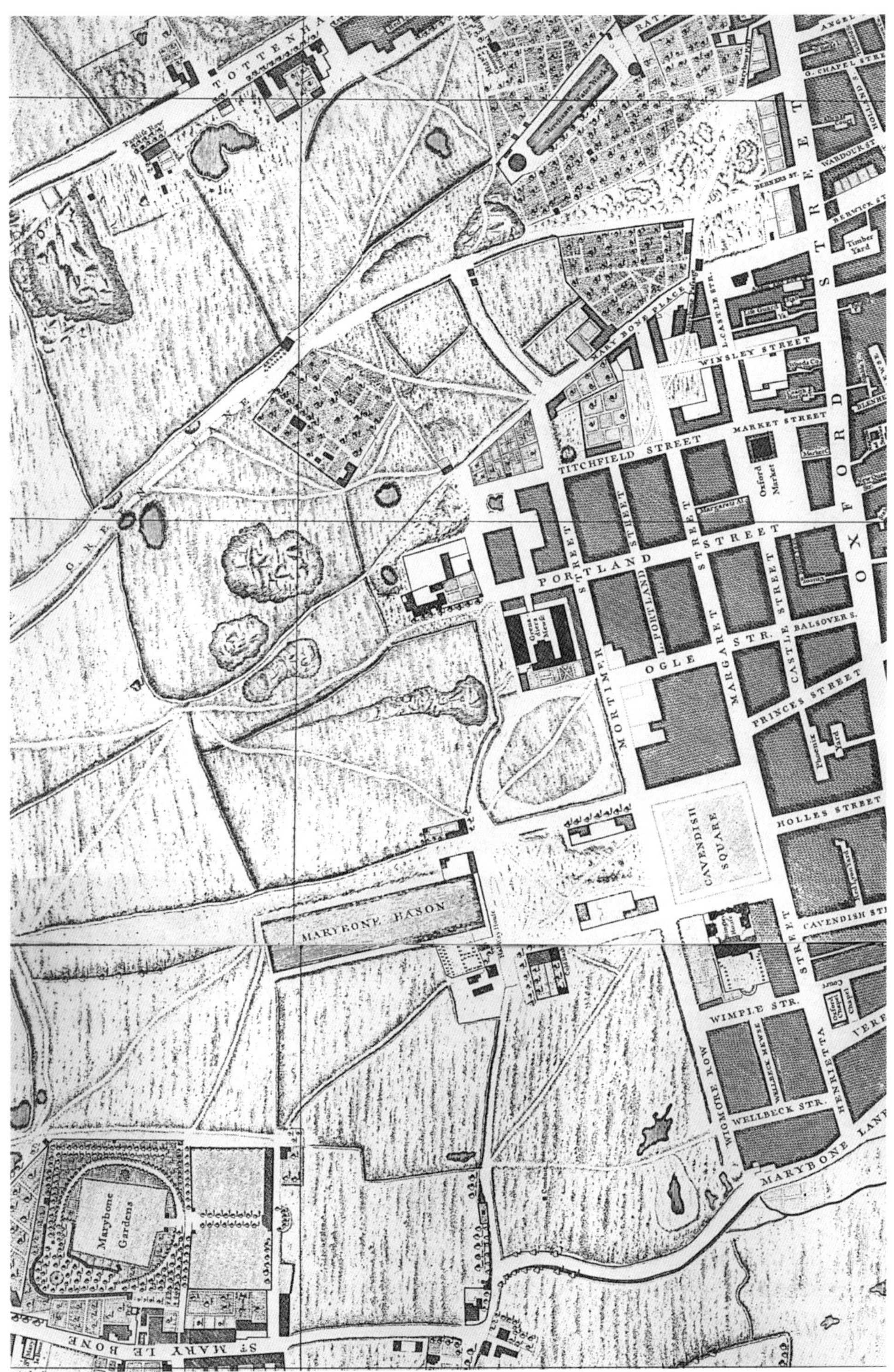

Section from John Rocque's map of London, 1746. (From the reprint by the London Topographical Society)

Introduction

Marylebone is a diverse and complex area of London comprising parts of W1, NW1 and NW8. It extends from Regent's Park and Lisson Green in the north, to Oxford Street in the south, and from Edgware Road in the west to a less exact line in the east which runs through Fitzrovia.

Famously, London is a city of villages: Marylebone in parts retains the feel of a small sophisticated town, especially around the High Street, while having many of the buildings, services, resources and historical associations of a city. But it also has a glorious park and one of the most famous shopping streets in the world in Oxford Street. And to the east there is the intimate and once raffish and artistic nature of Fitzrovia, an enclave divided between Marylebone and the old borough of St Pancras, and now between Westminster and Camden.

Marylebone also includes Tyburn, which was the original name of the village, derived from the stream which ran down to the Thames via Oxford Street. But Tyburn became synonymous only with the gallows near the site of Marble Arch and still powerfully denotes London's sinister and criminal past.

Marylebone contains some famous landmarks. They include the Wallace Collection, Madame Tussaud's, the Regent's Park terraces, Broadcasting House and also the fictional home of Sherlock Holmes.

Among its many famous residents have been Dr Johnson and his concupiscent crony, James Boswell; the novelist, Anthony Trollope; the unbalanced anti-Catholic demagogue Lord George Gordon; the historian Edward Gibbon, the actress Sarah Siddons and the Barretts (of Wimpole Street).

Marylebone shares in the dark or decadent history of London. In the eighteenth century, it housed a fair share of businesses providing the services of prostitutes – and at a higher level of affluence – the services of courtesans. They had little need to patrol the streets but instead serviced a rich clientele which paid generously for discretion, luxurious surroundings, and the skills of charming professional women. Some of these courtesans became very rich, making the most of years at the top of their profession.

Roque's map of 1746, published twenty years or so after the first grand developments took place, illustrates the essentially rural nature of the area. Apart from Cavendish Square, there is some residential development around Marylebone Lane, Wigmore Street, Henrietta Street (Place) and Welbeck Street and some houses are in the High Street near the pleasure ground, Marylebone Gardens. The map shows the old Marylebone manor house opposite the parish church: today, a plaque next to No. 60 Marylebone High Street records the site of the house. The rest of the district is virtually all fields, paths, lanes and hedges, so lacking in development that it was easy enough to build what became Marylebone Road through it in 1756.

A hundred years later Marylebone was transformed by the building of affluent squares and streets and the smaller roads which provided services and servants. It had acquired Regent's Park as a facility and as an adjunct, Portland Place, one of the widest roads in London which had the role of connecting the Prince Regent's Park to his Regent Street.

In contrast, the Lisson Grove area was predominantly working-class appealing to unskilled immigrants and others without much money. They were certainly no match for the Great Central Railway which deprived the area of many acres when it came into Marylebone station.

Significant historical footnotes are in this book such as the first omnibus service from Paddington to Bank, via the Yorkshire Stingo in Marylebone; the loss of life when the ice broke on Regent's Park lake in 1867; the Cato Street Conspiracy in 1820; the Balcombe Street Siege of 1975.

We have been much aided by the publications of the St Marylebone Society, which are recorded in Further Reading.

The Manors and the Tyburn River

In the Domesday Book of 1086, what is now St Marylebone consisted of two manors. To the east lay the manor of Tyburn, held by the Abbess of the convent of Barking under lease from the Crown. The Abbey, founded about 666, was used as a base by William I soon after his Conquest of 1066 and in gratitude he granted Tyburn to the Abbess. By the middle of the 12th century the manor was let to the de Sanford family for an annual rent of thirty shillings of which the monastery had the benefit until the Dissolution.

Gilbert de Sanford's daughter Alice inherited the lease of the manor when her father died in about 1250. She married Robert de Vere, Earl of Oxford and built the manor house, with a garden and a home farm some time before 1279.[1]

The other manor, known as 'Lilestone' or 'Lilleston', lay to the west, and was listed in Domesday Book as having eight families. In the reign of Edward the Confessor (*c*.1004-1066), it had apparently belonged to Edward, son of Swain, who was a servant of the King, but by the time of Domesday it was in the hands of Eideva, a woman of whom little is known but she may have been the head of a monastery. Lilestone is a corruption of 'Lille's tun' or farm and the name continues in the present-day Lisson Grove. Lilestone came into the hands of the Knights Templar. Originally established with the honourable intention of providing armed protection to Christian pilgrims making their way to the Holy Land, this order degenerated and its worldly wealth and increasing corruption led to its suppression in 1312 by the Crown. Lilestone then passed to another military order, the Knights of St John of Jerusalem. This is the origin of the name 'St John's Wood' which was then part of the Lilestone manor.

Geologically, Marylebone is divided into two distinct zones roughly bisected by the east- west Marylebone Road. To the north, are heavy London clays while the southern part is clay

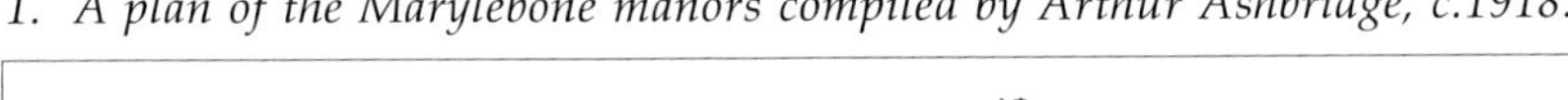

1. A plan of the Marylebone manors compiled by Arthur Ashbridge, c.1918.

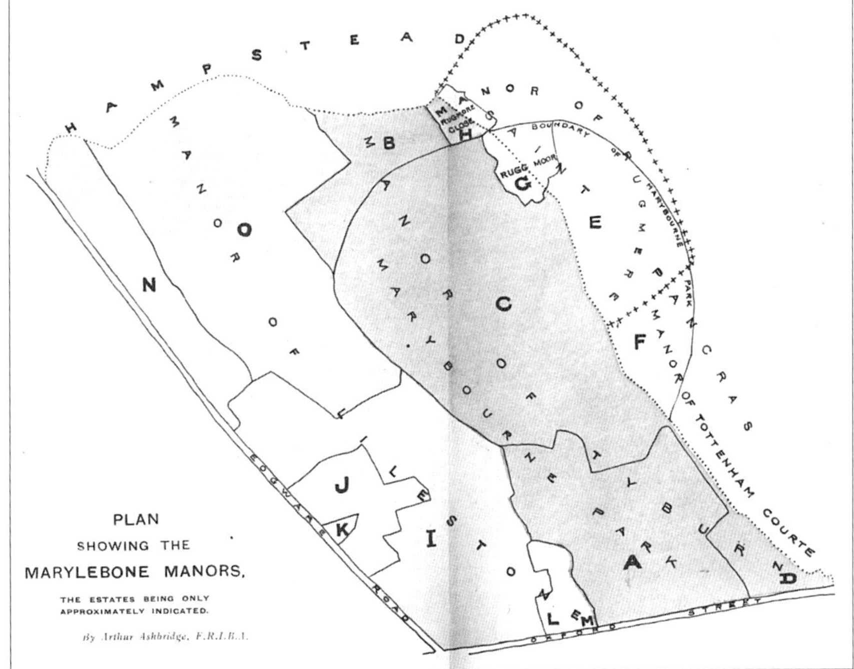

topped by gravel. As late as the sixteenth century, this meant that the northern part was hard to drain, lacked accessible water supplies and, therefore, was largely left as woodland and waste. The southern area, however, was well-drained and with available water supplies. Much of it was therefore cleared and brought into agricultural use. Consequently it features rather more in the scanty early history of Marylebone and Tyburn.

In 1200, a simple parish church, partly of timber, was built to serve the two manors. Dedicated to St John the Evangelist, it stood on the north side of the present Oxford Street close to the point at which the River Tyburn crossed, by the present day location of the Bond Street tube station. The village of Tyburn began there but gradually drifted north. This migration therefore left the church an isolated building which attracted robbers and vandals. Though the building was kept locked outside service times there were repeated depredations and the villagers eventually made representations to the Bishop of London, telling him that the old church "was in too lonely a place" and that "on account of the snares and plunderings of robbers, the books, vestments, images, bells, and other ornaments cannot be preserved as they should be nor divine service celebrated as is fitting"[2]

A new church was then constructed in about 1400 nearer the removed village of Tyburn and its manor house, about half a mile north up the Tyburn stream. It stood on the east side of the river and was dedicated to St Mary. The area and church became known as 'Marybourne' (1492) (bourne meaning stream), a name which eventually stabilised in the 17th century as Marylebone. The first recorded use of the prefix 'St' is in 1683. The name 'Tyburn' for the village gradually fell into disuse but continued to be used for the notorious gallows at the western end of Oxford Street.

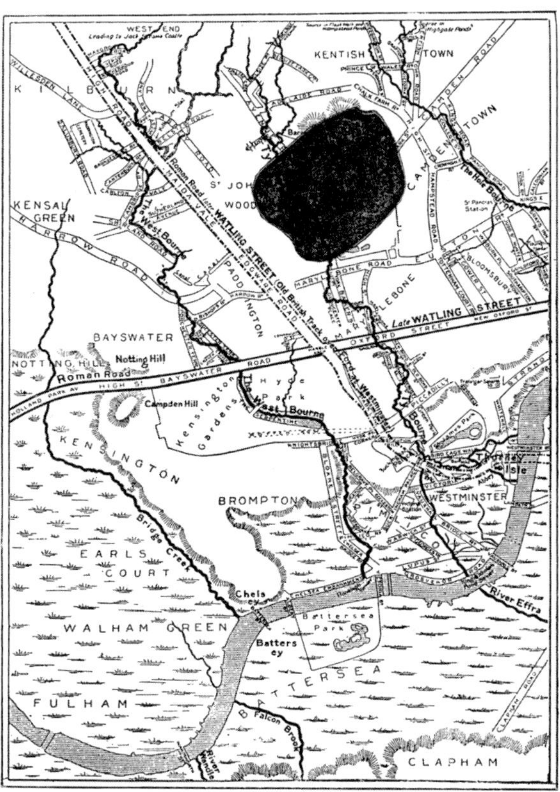

2. *The course of the River Tyburn from Hampstead down to the Thames, via Marylebone.*

SUCH A SMALL STREAM – SUCH A FAMOUS NAME

The eponymous stream has at various times been known as the Ty-bourne, Eye-bourn, Aye-brook and Teoburna, the name meaning 'boundary stream'. Near Oxford Street it acted as an approximate boundary between the two manors of Lileston and Tyburn – and south of Oxford Street it divides the manor of Ebury from the rest of Westminster. The Tyburn is a small and now almost entirely subterranean stream which rises at Shepherds Well by Fitzjohn's Avenue in the Lyndhurst Road area of Hampstead. Its water was then appreciated for its purity and enterprising hucksters sold it by the bucketful. It also provided sport for anglers. The river is joined by a small tributary which rises close to Hampstead Town Hall, flows through the Belsize Park district and skirts the western side of Primrose Hill. The combined stream crosses over the Regent's Canal in a cast-iron pipe aqueduct and picks up another small tributary that rises under London Zoo. Its route can be traced in the ornamental water in the west of Regent's Park close to Clarence Gate where it takes a sudden turn to the east. It then turns sharply south at York Gate, passing under Marylebone Road.

The bends of Marylebone High Street reflect the course of the Tyburn and a small depression in Oxford Street close to Stratford Place is also evidence of its hidden presence – maps by Morden and Lea dated respectively 1690 and 1700, show what is now Oxford Street crossing a nameless stream at this point. Aybrook Street, north of Blandford Street, takes its name from one of the river's old names.

In 1237, Gilbert de Sanford granted the City of London a strip of land on which was built the first stage of a conduit to take fresh water from the Tyburn springs to the City in order that "the rich and middling persons therein might have water for preparing their food and the poor for their drink". This was on the site of today's Stratford Place and from there the water pipes went south-east – hence Conduit Street, and then to the Strand and Fleet Street and the Great Conduit in Cheapside in the City. In 1875, workmen building a sewer in Stratford Place unearthed a stone structure which may have been associated with this initial conduit and was perhaps the first reservoir in London.

In 1565, a Banqueting House was built over the great storage cisterns there . This was used on occasions by members of the City Corporation who made annual inspections of the conduits. In 1613 the New River, taking its supplies from Hertfordshire, began to supply (for a fee) the northern parts of the City, but it was slow to displace the reliance on free conduits and springs. Therefore the Banqueting House continued to be used by the City fathers who hunted hares and foxes in the vicinity and then restored themselves with food and drink. The building was demolished *c.* 1755 when Stratford Place was built on the site.

3. The Banqueting House, on the site of today's Stratford Place.

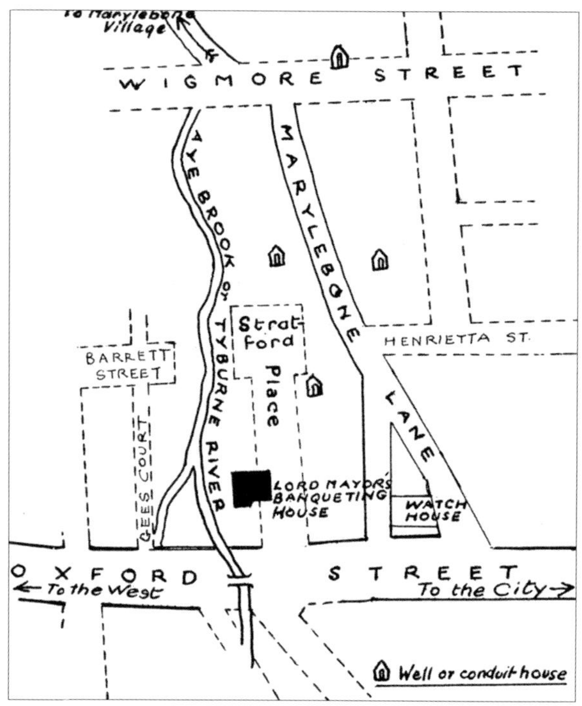

4. Site of the old Tyburn village and of the Banqueting House. Subsequently Stratford Place was built there.

5. Marylebone Manor House in the High Street.

CHANGES OF OWNERSHIP

By the 13th century and by the marriage of Alice de Sanford to Robert de Vere, virtually the whole of the manors of Tyburn and Lilestone were owned by him. In 1312, they became the property of Alice's grandson, John de Warrenne, Earl of Surrey and Sussex. He died without issue and they passed to his nephew Richard and later to his son, also Richard. By 1415, the manor of Tyburn was divided amongst three daughters of the second Richard.

Before 1500, the Lord of Tyburn manor was a senior civil servant of Henry VII, Thomas Hobson, of unknown antecedents, but of considerable skill and ability. As well as being a man of influence and position, Hobson made several purchases of land in the area so that before his death in 1511, he had acquired the greater part of the manor.[3]

He left money to the "high aulter of Marybone" and the manor of Marybone and the house to his wife Joan for her life, and thereafter to their son Richard. From the high value which he placed on the manor house in his will, it may be that he had enlarged or rebuilt it. The manor was inherited by Hobson's grandson, also Thomas.

Henry VIII's ruthless dissolution of the monasteries changed the history of the parish. His acquisition of lands formerly owned by monasteries, included Marylebone Park. He appropriated the thirty shillings a year rent due to Barking Abbey, but he also wanted to acquire the interest in the land owned by the young Thomas Hobson so as to expand his nearby hunting grounds.

In about 1539, the king acquired the manor from Hobson (who was then only eighteen), as part of an exchange whereby young Thomas got land on the Isle of Wight and houses in Southampton. The manor house was located at the northern end of the High Street, on the east side opposite the parish church. Having been acquired by Henry VIII, the house become a royal hunting lodge. The house was used as a boys' school at the beginning of the 18th century before being demolished in 1791.

The Portman family acquired much of the Manor of Lilestone in 1533 when Sir William Portman, Lord Chief Justice to Henry VIII, bought the freehold of 270 acres of land – his name is still familiar today in street names. The land remained largely undeveloped until 1755 when residential development began.

GOD MADE THE COUNTRY...

The so-called 'Agas' map of London of *c*.1560 illustrates the rural aspect of Marylebone: the area north of Oxford Street (then named 'the road to Uxbridge') is open country of fields, hedges and trees. Few landmarks were visible to the traveller, other than the church of Mary-le-Bourne, some scattered houses, the manor house and the gallows at Tyburn. It is likely that arable land extended over what is now Cavendish Square and that cattle grazed on pasture later Wigmore Street and Portman Square. The cottagers' pigs snuffled in the oak and beech woods stretching away to the north. And when the King of Muscovy's hunting party galloped across Marylebone Park in 1601, the village of Mary-le-Bourne was surrounded by fields.

6. *The 'Agas' map of c. 1560 included a part of Marylebone. A section shows at the foot the 'road to Uxbridge' – today's Oxford Street. Going north is what is now Tottenham Court Road.*

To the south of the parish along the main road to London, now Oxford Street, there was a regular flow of traffic including livestock for sale or slaughter at Smithfield. Market days, which sometimes coincided with execution days at Tyburn (usually a Monday, so the condemned had the benefit of a Sunday service), caused huge congestion.

The expansion of London reached Marylebone at the beginning of the 18th century. The village was about to grow up.

[1] Ann Saunders, *Regent's Park from 1086 to the present* (rev. edn. 1981), 17.

[2] *Ibid* 17

[3] *Ibid* 18

Tyburn Fair

Long before significant development took place in Marylebone, the gallows at Tyburn at the junction of the present Oxford Street and Edgware Road were widely known as a place of public execution. From the late 12th century to its removal in 1783, tens of thousands of people died at the 'Fatal Tree'.

EARLY EXECUTIONS

One of the earliest known executions at Tyburn was that of William FitzOsbert who, in 1196, was accused of sedition for leading a revolt of merchants and artisans protesting at the payment of taxes levied to raise money for the ransom for Richard I (the Lionheart) (r. 1189-1199) – the king had been captured in Austria on his return from the Crusades. Thousands of executions followed over the next six centuries including – at random – Roger Mortimer, the lover of Queen Isabella in 1329, Roger Bolingbroke for attempting the regicide of Henry VI by sorcery in the 1440s, the pretender Perkin Warbeck in 1499, the 'Holy Maid of Kent', Elizabeth Barton, in 1534, Thomas Culpepper in 1541 who had been incriminated in an affair with Henry VIII's wife, Catherine Howard .

THE 'TRIPLE TREE'

The triangular gallows, the 'Triple Tree', was built in 1571, capable of hanging up to twenty-four people at a time – eight on each beam. The first person to be executed on it was John Story, convicted of treason for conspiring to murder the Queen and for informing the Spanish on how to invade England. It was recorded that: 'the saide Story was drawn upon a herdell from the Tower of London unto Tiborn, where was prepared for him a newe payre of gallows made in triangular maner' (*Harleian Misc.* iii. 1809: 100-8). It was also noted that Story summoned sufficient strength to strike a blow at the executioner just as the latter was about to disembowel him.

7. *An execution at Tyburn during the Tudor period.*

FAMOUS EXECUTIONS

During the reign of Elizabeth I (*r.*1558-1603), many Catholics died on the gallows, because of their choice of faith. Their deaths were commemorated by the establishment in 1910 of the Tyburn Convent on Bayswater Road. The Convent keeps relics of some of the Catholics who died there. In 1678, following (false) allegations made by Titus Oates of a Catholic plot, a wave of anti-Catholic persecution resulted, thirty-five innocent people being executed.

In January 1661, the body of Oliver Cromwell, who had died in September 1658, was exhumed and ritually hanged and then decapitated at Tyburn along with Henry Ireton (his son-in-law who had died in 1651) and John Bradshaw (d. 1659), the presiding judge at the trial of Charles I. The remains of the three corpses were thrown into a pit near the gallows.

8. The execution of Lord Ferrers at Tyburn in 1760.

Other notables who made their last journey from Newgate Prison to Tyburn included Jonathan Wild (1725), London's first master of the underworld, the popular burglar and escapologist Jack Sheppard in 1724 and Lord Ferrers in 1760, the first nobleman to be executed on the Tyburn gallows. Ferrers, convicted of murdering an old and faithful family retainer John Johnson, assumed that his peers in the House of Lords would acquit him but the crime and his reputation as a bully overcame class loyalty. Crowds gathered to jeer him on his way to Tyburn in a black coach and wearing a white satin wedding suit.

THE DEATH OF CATHERINE HAYES
Catherine Hayes suffered a harrowing execution in 1726. Hayes worked alternately as a prostitute and domestic servant. Her reputation in the district was that of quick tempered shrew. In 1713, she married John Hayes although she took other lovers within months of the marriage and tiring of her husband, she planned to kill him with the help of two of her lovers. In 1725, these two men, Thomas Billings and Thomas Wood, killed John with an axe. They dismembered him throwing some of the pieces of his body into a

pond in Marylebone Fields. The head was otherwise disposed of. Catherine and her lovers were arrested. Billings and Wood were sentenced to be hanged at Tyburn and their bodies to be gibbeted – hanged in chains – while Catherine was to be burned alive at the stake. Wood died in prison of gaol fever. A huge crowd gathered at Tyburn in May 1726. Three men condemned for sodomy, three highwaymen and two burglars, accompanied Billings in the cart from Newgate, while Hayes was drawn to Tyburn on a hurdle. She was the last woman to be executed in England for 'petty treason', an offence which dated back to the 14th century, that involved the crime of the killing of a master by a servant and likewise the killing of a man by his spouse.

At Tyburn, the three carts were positioned under the beams, the condemned made their devotions, and the carts were moved leaving the men suspended. Hayes, who had witnessed the executions, was secured to a stake a few yards from the gallows. Brushwood was piled around her. Terrified, she begged the hangman to strangle her. He tried to pull the cord around her neck, but the flames blew in his direction and he retreated. She was, indeed, burned alive.

THE TYBURN FAIR

The eight Tyburn execution days were a fixture in the calendar and Tyburn Fair – the day of execution and the customs surrounding it – was a popular spectacle, holiday and gruesome wake. William Hogarth depicted it thus in his *The Idle 'Prentice at Tyburn.* His image shows a throng of people awaiting the execution, the condemned and the prison ordinary in the cart with the gallows looming in the distance.

Execution day guaranteed crowds of thousands especially if the victims included felons whose crimes were notorious. Onlookers assembled along the route from Newgate, through Holborn and St Giles and along what is now Oxford Street to the gallows, many following the procession westwards. The procession stopped occasionally en route for drink: some prisoners were succoured sufficiently by the alcohol to anticipate calmly the death awaiting them at Tyburn. A prison chaplain rode with the condemned exhorting them to shrive their sins by confession and make peace with their Lord.

Prisoners who addressed the crowd from the gallows were appreciated. Around the gallows, the crowd was densely packed. The better-off hired seats in a purpose-built grandstand. Those who had the ringside seats might have arrived many hours earlier. Many would sit or stand on the walls then enclosing Hyde Park for a better view while others resorted to ladders.

Samuel Johnson's friend James Boswell reflected in his *London Journal* of 1763 on a visit to Tyburn: 'My curiosity to see the melancholy spectacle of the executions was so strong that I could not resist it … I got upon a scaffold very near the fatal tree, so that we could clearly see the dismal scene.' He commented on a 'most prodigious crowd of spectators'. After the execution he admitted that he was 'most horribly shocked, and thrown into a very deep melancholy' by the whole experience but admitted that 'it is a weakness of mind. I own it'.

THE MOVABLE SCAFFOLD

A movable scaffold was introduced in 1759. The *Whitehall Evening Post* of 4 October recorded that at half past nine in the morning 'four malefactors were carried in two carts from Newgate and executed on the new Moving Gallows at Tyburn.' The *Gentleman's Magazine* 29 August 1783 wrote that the movable gallows were 'fixed about 50 yards nearer the Park wall than usual.'

THE ANATOMISTS

As medicine became a profession, dead bodies were needed for study: they were, in short, valuable. One source of these were the poor wretches hanged at Tyburn unless friends or relatives could prevent it. The accounts of the Company of Barber-Surgeons describe the intensity of the conflict around the scaffold as the claimants for the corpses competed:

> '1717 Paid my Lord Chief Justice Parkers Tipstaffe for taking four Dead Bodies from Tyburn this year – expenses £2.8.0.
>
> 1720 Paid the hangman for the dead mans clothes which were lost in the scuffle and for his Christmas Box £0.15.0.
>
> 1740 Paid for mending the windows broke upon bringing the last body from Tyburn £0.6.0.'

Bernard Mandeville, writing in 1725, commented on the scene following an execution:

> '… the next Entertainment is a squabble between the surgeons and the Mob, about the dead bodies … They have suffer'd the Law (cries the rabble) and shall have no other barbarities put upon them … If the others are numerous and resolute enough to persist in this Enterprise, a Fray ensues.'

Objects were thrown at the executioner and other officials and attempts were made to seize the hanging felon either to kill him quickly by pulling on his legs or to rescue his corpse. Relatives and friends of the condemned travelled to the gallows to claim the body. John Casey, who rode with his brother in the cart in 1721, managed to protect his corpse. The brother and sister of Matthew Lee came from Lincoln for the same purpose. Oliver White's father journeyed from Carlisle to protect his son's grave over night. In 1731, the father of Samuel Curlis walked thirty miles to see him hanged at Tyburn, taking possession of his body afterwards. Sailors accounted for nearly twenty-five-per cent of the condemned in the 18th century at Tyburn: riots involving sailors trying to recover the bodies of fellow sailors were recorded on at least twelve occasions. There was growing concern that such actions threatened public order.

Today, a plaque in the traffic island at the junction of Edgware Road and Bayswater Road reminds us of this tumultuous, even overwhelming, scene. The Masons Arms in Upper Berkeley Street claims that it is situated on the site of the dungeon where prisoners were held before their hanging. On the cellar walls are fittings allegedly used as manacles for the prisoners.

THE SITE

The exact site of the gallows is debatable. Although a plaque marks the site in the traffic island, other claims have been made, to wit, the house in the south-east corner of Connaught Square, formerly 49. A writer in *The Antiquary* in October 1873, noted,

> 'I was born within 100 yards of the exact spot on which the gallows stood, and my uncle took up the stones on which the uprights were placed … In 1810, when Connaught Place was being built, he was employed on the works.'

The writer adds that his mother remembered the posts standing when she was a child as she was born in Bryanston Street. She stated that when Connaught Square was being built, she saw quantities of human bones being taken away. She added that old inhabitants of the neighbourhood in about 1750 claimed that the area from the toll-house to Frederick Mews was used as a place of execution, and the bodies buried adjacent. When executions came to an end at Tyburn it was said that the gallows were bought by a carpenter who made them into stands for beer-butts in the cellars of the nearby Carpenters' Arms public-house.

When the fixed triangular gallows was removed in the 1750s this was followed by the occupation of the site by the toll-house, which had been moved from the east corner of Park Lane, then called Tyburn Lane, to the corner of Edgware Road.

THE RURAL GALLOWS

The gallows have been depicted in a number of maps and illustrations from the 17th century. Camden's *Britannia* (1607), shows them as a triangular structure outside the north-eastern angle of Hyde Park. Despite the expansion of London during the 18th century the Norwich-born artist, William Capon, depicts Tyburn's rural location in a sketch made in 1785, two years after the last execution. The scene looks towards Hyde Park from the last house on Seymour Place. In the forefront on the right hand side is a gallery from which people viewed the spectacle. Behind the gallery there is a fence which encloses a barnyard and a cow in a field.

FASHIONABLE DEVELOPMENT

Development of the fashionable districts of Marylebone began in the 1720s and residents would have been aware of the large crowds lining Oxford Street on execution days. It was estimated that some 200,000 thronged the route to see Jack Sheppard hanged in 1724. The noise, smells, and rowdiness of the crowds on Tyburn Fair days jarred with the atmosphere of an expensive residential development attracting residents accustomed to position. But it was not until 29 August 1783 that the last executions occurred – either William Ryland, a forger, or John Austin had the dubious distinction of being the final victims. Executions were then transferred to the street outside Newgate Prison where the crowds could be more easily controlled.

Dr Johnson lamented their removal:

> If they do not draw spectators, they do not answer their purpose. The old method was most satisfactory for all parties: the public was gratified by a procession; the criminal was supported by it. Why has all this to be swept away?'

The Portland Estate

THE HARLEYS, THE PORTLANDS AND THE HOWARD DE WALDEN ESTATE

Today, the Howard de Walden Estate owns and leases over 90 acres of real estate in Marylebone from Marylebone High Street in the west to Portland Place in the east and from Wigmore Street in the south to Marylebone Road in the north. When the 5th Duke of Portland died in 1879, land passed in the female line to the duke's sister, Lucy Joan Bentinck (1807-1899), widow of the 6th Baron Howard de Walden. The Portland Estate then became the Howard de Walden Estate.

At the close of the 17th century, Marylebone was a small village of not many more than a hundred houses. In 1728 the *Daily Journal* commented that people were arriving in London from their "country houses" in Marylebone. The transformation from village to part of central London commenced shortly after the accession of George I to the throne in 1714. The century saw the development of the fashionable squares from which emanated elegant residential streets such as Portland Place. There were two slumps, from about 1720 to 1730 and again from 1801 to 1811 when building more or less came to a standstill, the first time due to an economic depression and the second, the effect of the wars with Napoleon.

The façades of the houses reflected the architectural proportions of neo-classical architecture, whose chief proponent in England had been Lord Burlington (1694-1753). Where the houses were arranged around a square, the front elevations were sometimes planned as symmetrical, while in others the buildings were individually developed under leases. Montagu House (destroyed 1940), set at a 45-degree angle on the north-west corner of Portman Square, was an obtrusive exception to the rule.

The first of the squares, Cavendish, was on the then Harley Cavendish Estate (commenced in 1719), followed by Portman (1764-84), Manchester (1776-78), Montagu (1811), Dorset (1787 to 1811) and Bryanston (1824).

The system for obtaining permission to develop the land was as follows. The Lord of the manor (the freeholder) secured a licence from the monarch, who could grant or withhold it at will – and if he granted it, he could secure certain conditions. Later, the licence was replaced by consent via a private Act of Parliament. The plan, once approved, would then be implemented in a number of ways. The Lord could grant a building lease with a low ground rent, the builder then being the lessee and could with consent grant a sub-lease on completion of the house. Upon reversion of the lease, of course, the lord of the manor retained the house. An alternative was to grant a lease for a specified period (initially this was shorter than 99 years) and the lessee would, according to an approved plan, build his house. Another alternative was for the Lord to be the builder, taking the capital risk and then granting a lease.

In any case, the estate owner took a ground rent and retained the freehold which, generally, was entailed on the eldest male heir. By this method, the large estates were kept intact. In 1870 the estate holder was entitled to sell land, retaining instead the capital in trust for the beneficiary of the entailment. The expiration of the 99-year leases has permitted, on the granting of a new leasehold, approval of plans for re-facing or even entire demolition or rebuilding of individual houses. This resulted in interesting new visual effects, particularly, for example, in Harley, Wigmore and Wimpole Streets.

At the time of development in the 18th century the two principal landowners in the parish were the Duke of Portland and, to the west, the Portman family.

THE PORTLAND ESTATE

In *c.*1710, the Austen family sold the village and manor of Tyburn to John Holles, Duke of Newcastle. His only daughter (and heiress) Henrietta Cavendish Holles, brought this estate to her marriage with Edward Harley in 1713. Harley was the son of the 1st Earl of Oxford and Mortimer. Harley (1688-1741) became the 2nd Earl in 1724. He died, owing creditors £375,000

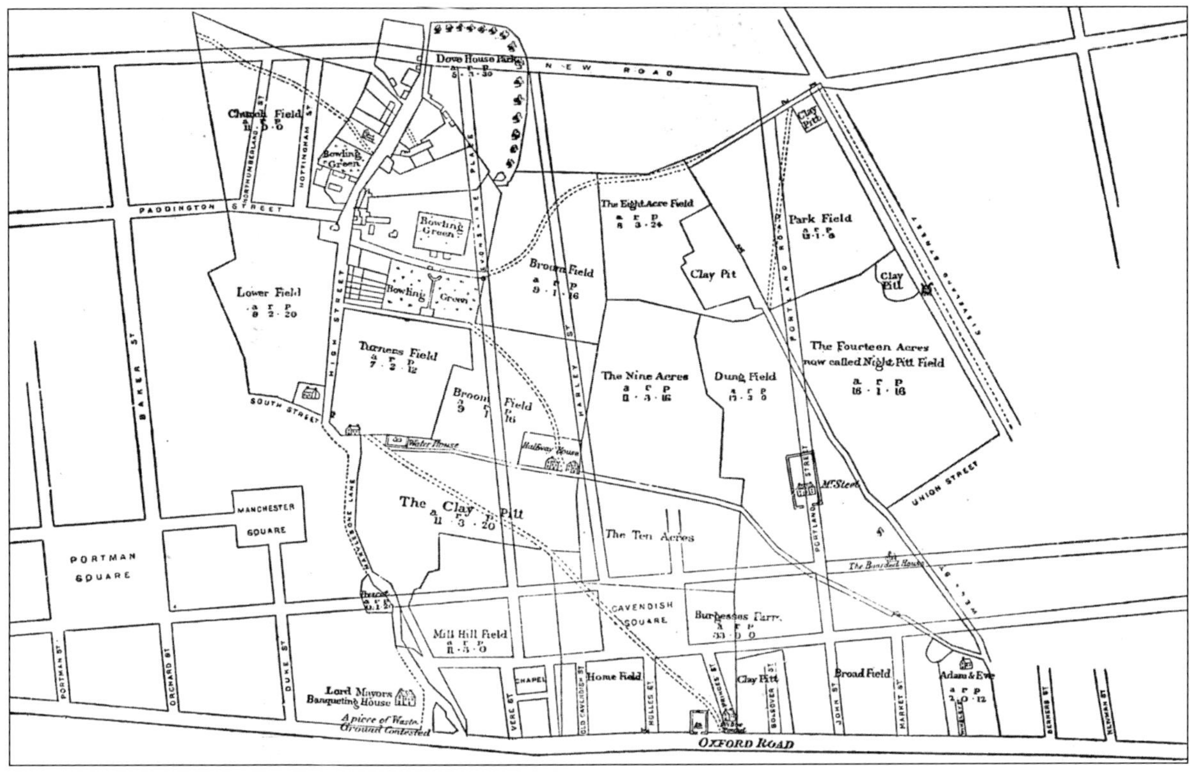

9. *The Marylebone Estate when purchased by the Duke of Newcastle c. 1710.*

and a complex estate which included a famous library. To store the vast number of books, his trustees purchased a house in Marylebone High Street, later realising it was too small for the purpose. Among Harley's creditors was William Thomas, owed a substantial sum.[1] One hopes that this long-serving loyal and remarkable servant of the Harleys, whose services to the parish are described on p. 125, was paid.

Henrietta and Edward's only child, Margaret Cavendish Bentinck (née Harley) (1715–1785), married the 2nd Duke of Portland (known as the handsomest man in England) in 1734 and when she inherited the Harley Estate it then passed to the Portlands.

The early ownership of this estate is reflected in some street names – Henrietta Place, Cavendish Square, Holles Street, Harley Street, Mortimer Street, Margaret Street. One of the Earl of Oxford's titles was Lord Harley of Wigmore, and their country seat in Cambridgeshire was Wimpole Hall. Duchess Street and Great Portland Street also remember this aristocratic past.

CAVENDISH SQUARE AND ITS ENVIRONS

The plans by John Prince of 1719 for the Cavendish Square Estate showed an area around the Square stretching from Oxford Street in the south to New Cavendish Street in the north, Marylebone Lane to the west and what is now Wells Street to the east. Edward Harley, interested in other matters including his library, handed over the supervision of the development to his uncle also named Edward Harley, a Tory Member of Parliament. The early list of those who were willing to build on the estate consists entirely of Tory grandees: Lord Dartmouth, a secretary of State, Lord Carnarvon, Lord Harcourt, and Lord Bingley, a Lord Chancellor.

North of Cavendish Square the plan specified another square to be called Queen Anne. This did not materialise for reasons we shall later

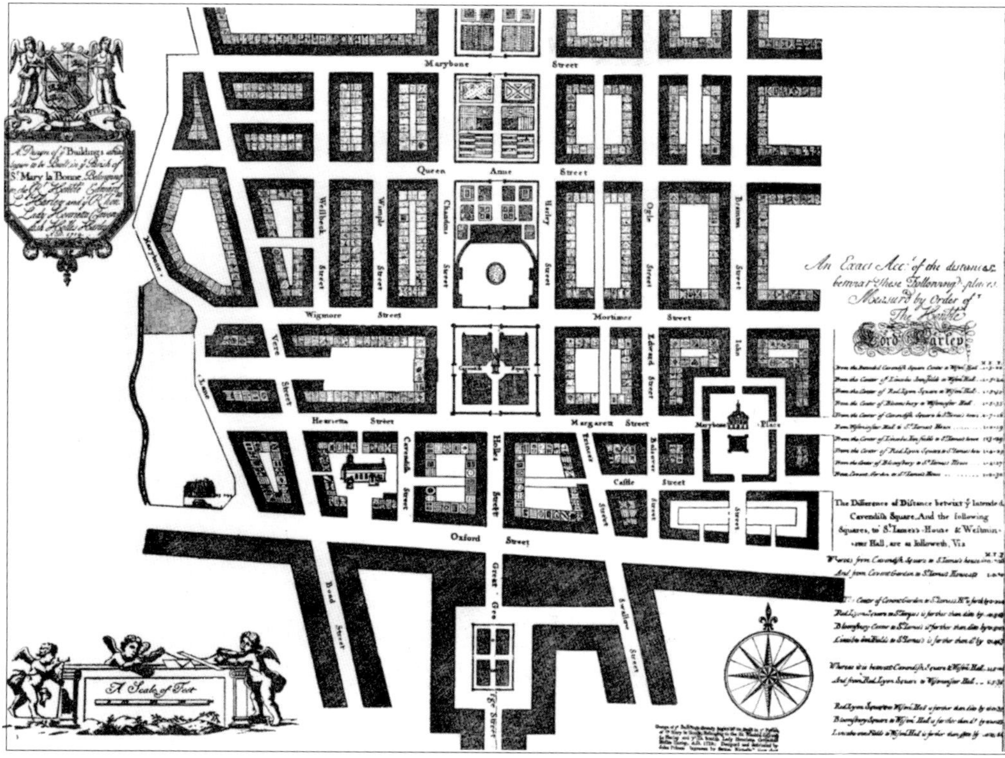

10. *Plan drawn up by John Prince for the development of the Harley Estate in 1719.*

11. *Edward Harley, 2nd Earl of Oxford. Oil, c. 1725, attributed to Jonathan Richardson.*

describe. Lord Carnarvon, later Duke of Chandos acquired the freehold of land to the north of Cavendish Square from the Harleys in 1723.[2] Evidence for this is a modern development (1966-1970) on the west side of Harley Street, just before the junction with Queen Anne Street. There was bomb damage from the Second World War on the site; the freeholder (not the Howard de Walden Estate) permitted the development, which is obtrusive and unsympathetic.

Lords Bingley and Harcourt took building leases and the architect and surveyor were James Gibbs (1682-1784) and John Prince respectively. Prince acted as an agent, but also speculated on his own account, calling himself 'Prince of Builders'.[3] The plans showed a spacious Cavendish Square just north of Oxford Street accessed via Holles Street and included a chapel and a market (the Oxford Market). In short, the plan followed the pattern established in Hanover Square and St. James's Square.

12. *The north side of Cavendish Square, c. 1800, by Thomas Malton. The corner houses were built for the Duke of Chandos, and the twin mansions in the centre, which still survive, were built in the 1770s by a Mr Tuffnell.*

Building was due to start in 1720, but when the South Sea Company failed many of its investors were ruined. This caused a financial crash and in turn stalled the development of the Square for years. The lack of progress and poor physical state of the Square was noted in the *New Critical Review of the Public Buildings of London* in 1736:

I am morally assured that more people are displeased at seeing this square lie in its present neglected condition than are entertained with what was meant for elegance or ornament in it.'

The Duke of Chandos (then Earl of Carnarvon), one of the richest men in England, was not spared criticism either. It was noted that the Duke might now 'ride from town to the country through his own estate (between Cavendish Square and his palace of Canons at Edgware).' The Duke may have been prevented from proceeding with his own plans on the north side of the Square as he too had been affected by the South Sea Bubble, but he did build two houses, one on the north-west corner (which survives) and one on the north-east corner, which does not. The space between those two houses remained vacant until 1770 when a Mr. Tuffnell built a pair of houses. John Summerson, in *Georgian London* concludes that the designs for those two houses are so grandiose that they may have been taken over from the Society of Dilettanti,[4] which had previously acquired the leasehold intending to build, but abandoned their plans. The buildings now form the Convent of the Holy Child Jesus linked by an arch bearing a sculpture by Jacob Epstein entitled *Madonna and Child* (1950).

Chandos lived in the house on the west corner with Harley Street (no 16) from 1736 to 1744.

Daniel Defoe (1660-1731), commenting on the expansion of west London in the 1720s, said that it was a 'world full of bricklayers and labourers.' Over a century later Thomas Babington Macaulay (1800-1859), speaking before Parliament on 2 March 1831, described the development north of Oxford Street as probably superior in 'opulence, intelligence, and general respectability, to any city in the world.'[5]

The Oxford Market designed by James Gibbs,[6]

13. *A closer look at the twin mansions on the north side of Cavendish Square. A photograph c. 1926.*

14. *Oxford Market, originally designed by Gibbs.*

just to the east of Great Portland Street, opened in 1731 and continued selling meat, fish and vegetables until it was demolished in 1876. The row of houses on the north side of Oxford Street was completed in 1729 and the development of the streets leading to Cavendish Square and Oxford Market – Henrietta, Vere, Holles, Margaret, Cavendish, Welbeck, Wimpole Princes, Bolsover, Castle and Market Streets – followed. In addition, the ground was laid out for Lower Harley Street (after 1866 joined with Upper Harley Street, to become only Harley Street, and definitively re-numbered at that time), Wigmore Street and Mortimer Street.

William Maitland whose *History of London* was published in 1739, wrote that there were 577 houses in the parish of Marylebone, and 35 persons who kept coaches, but still by the middle of the century the area was dominated by fields. John Rocque's 1746 map of London shows building only as far north as Wigmore Street and on the east side of Great Portland Street to Mortimer Street. Even later in the century, Oxford

15. *Harcourt House, 1838, surrounded by its enormously high wall, built to preserve the privacy of the eccentric 5th Duke of Portland.*

Street had houses only on its southern side between New Bond Street and the Tyburn Turnpike (now Park Lane), many of which were described as being occupied by 'dustmen, chimney-sweepers, and purveyors of asses milk.'

During the 1760s, the pace increased. The development around Cavendish Square was intended for those with taste and money. At the same time many of the labourers and craftsmen employed in the construction settled in the poorer eastern end of Oxford Street and the Marylebone vestrymen were anxious to monitor their numbers lest their residence render them entitled to poor relief paid for by the householders of the parish.

The financial success from the rental of property on the Harley Estate was a long time coming. In 1721, the income was only £186, by 1768, £4786, about £128,000 in today's money.[7]

THE GARDENS OF CAVENDISH SQUARE
The design of the Square by Charles Bridgeman showed a central green space set inside railings with a planned statue of Queen Anne, but this was not erected. Instead, in 1770, an equestrian statue of William Augustus, Duke of Cumberland (1721–1765), commander of His Majesty's forces in the bloody and decisive battle of Culloden in 1746, was placed there until its removal in 1868. The stone base, with its inscription, remains.

On the south side of the gardens is a statue of Lord William George Frederick Cavendish Scott-Bentinck (1802-1848), a devotee of the turf, and second surviving son of the 4th Duke of Portland. The work dates from 1851 and was sculpted by Thomas Campbell. Scott-Bentinck had a short but influential life in politics, encouraged by his uncle George Canning; he opposed the free trade laws and assisted in bringing down the government of Sir Robert Peel.

The present design of the gardens dates from l971 when Westminster City Council built a car park beneath the Square and installed the (unsuitable) brick wall and railing.

THE HOUSES OF CAVENDISH SQUARE
Harcourt House (demolished 1903), which occupied the largest portion of the west side, was built originally for Lord Bingley in 1722 to the design of Thomas Archer. The lease was purchased in 1773 by the 3rd Lord Harcourt, a grandson of the Harcourt who had originally

leased and built on the east side of the Square. The Earl lost the house in 1825, while gambling, to the 5th Duke of Portland (1800-1879). The reclusive Duke *(see p.121)* built a wall of opaque glass and cast-iron 200 feet long and 80 feet high at the back, a determined attempt to maintain his privacy. Harcourt House lay semi-derelict for many years before its demolition, when it was rebuilt as flats, faced in Portland stone. Also called Harcourt House they are located at numbers 19 and 19A.

The southern side of Cavendish Square comprised large private houses, but these were demolished and redeveloped over the years, particularly in the 1970s, so that this side of the Square is more closely linked with Oxford Street than originally and the scale very different. Much of it now forms the rear elevation of the John Lewis department store, rebuilt after the last war. The scale of the store is imposing, but viewed as one walks south down Harley Street, with its set-back upper storey and roundel windows on either side, it has purposeful elegance.

Immediately to the north of Cavendish Square between Queen Anne Street and Weymouth Street was a large reservoir known as the Marylebone Basin, which by the 18th century was a place for bathing and also supplied the waterworks at Buckingham Palace and the York Buildings Waterworks in the Strand, established in 1696. The Basin was drained between 1764-6, giving way to the development around Mansfield Street, and Portland Place. The failure of the Duke of Chandos to build his grand house on the north side of Cavendish Square may have derived from a wish to make money from the water supply in the Basin.

The draining of the Basin allowed the building by Robert and James Adam of Chandos House at 2 Queen Anne Street, between 1769 and 1771. Chandos House and Home House (20 Portman Square) are two of the four finest examples of their work in London. The interior of Chandos House is an Adam arrangement of light-filled grandeur.

An unobstructed view of Chandos House is

16. Houses in Wigmore Street (then Wigmore Row), a watercolour by T H Shepherd.

17. Chandos House in Queen Anne Street.

afforded by standing in the north-east corner of Cavendish Square looking north into Chandos Place. The façade is an imposing spare neo-classical design faced in Scottish Craigleith stone. The portico and columns supporting it reward an observer at close range: the capitals of the columns are decorated with an acanthus pattern in low relief and the portico with the signature Adam device of rams' heads, linked by husk garlands.

The house was built as a speculative venture on a 99-year lease from the 2nd Duke of Portland.[8] The Adam brothers then sold the lease in 1774 to James Brydges, the 3rd and last Duke of Chandos for the sum of £11,000.

The Duke and Duchess did not live in the very grand main state rooms saved for public display, but instead in the rear wing which could be closed off from the main house and had its own plain staircase.

Following the Duke's death the house passed to his second wife, her estate being managed by trustees. On her death on 20 January 1813, the leasehold passed to her daughter Anna Eliza. Her husband, Richard Temple, leased the property and from 1815 to 1871 the lessee was the Austro-Hungarian Empire whose Embassy it was. The first Ambassador, Prince Esterhazy, entertained on a lavish scale to the envy of the US ambassador who pleaded with US Congress for funds to compete.

In 1866, the 3rd Duke of Buckingham and Chandos acquired the reversionary lease and he lived there after the expiration of the lease to the Embassy, before appointment as Governor of Madras in 1875. Other titled families took over the lease including the Countess of Strafford in 1905 and in 1924 the Earl of Shaftesbury who modernised the property. The newspaper proprietor Sir James Gomer Berry, Viscount Kemsley (1927-1957), was the last to use Chandos House as a private residence.

Lady Focke, granddaughter of Lord Kemsley spent time with her governess at Chandos, and remembers dark and cold formality, the public rooms being out of bounds. She recalls there being approximately twelve staff many of whom were long-serving and some of them, regardless of their actual names, being called by a particular name: the footman, for example, was always 'William'. Lady Kemsley employed a French chef René and the menus for entertainments were handwritten in French.

The house suffered bomb damage in the Second World War, but was restored in the 1950s. In 1964, the lease was granted to the Royal Society of Medicine who restored the building. The RSM sold the lease in August 1986, and the house then passed through a succession of owners; it remained empty and neglected to growing concern for the interiors and vulnerable fittings and indeed certain of the original mantelpieces were stolen. In 2002, the Howard de Walden Estate stepped in to save the building by acquiring the lease and carrying out urgent repairs. Working with English Heritage, the Estate then restored Chandos before granting a new lease to the Royal Society of Medicine. The recent restoration, using archaeological techniques, has revealed that painted pastoral vignettes commissioned by the Adam brothers were by Antonio Zucchi (1726-1795) and not,

18. *Herbert Asquith, a resident of No. 20 Cavendish Square.*

as some had speculated, by Zucchi's more famous wife, Angelica Kauffmann.

Chandos House is a Grade I listed building.

SOME NOTABLE INHABITANTS

At No. 5, on the south-east side lived *Quintin Hogg* (1845-1903) *(see p. 65)*, merchant and philanthropist, between 1885 and 1898, later selling the house and moving to an apartment in Stratford Place.

At No. 20 (on the south-west corner) from 1905 to 1908 lived *Henry Herbert Asquith* (1852-1928), 1st Earl of Oxford and Asquith, later Prime Minister.

At No. 18, *Sir Ronald Ross* (1857–1932), Nobel Laureate and the discoverer of the mosquito transmission of malaria, was a resident.

At No. 14 (the north-east corner) lived *George E. Street*, (1824-1881), architect of the Law Courts in the Strand.

Probably at No. 19[9] – the remarkable, fascinating and ascerbic writer, *Lady Mary Wortley Montagu* (1689-1762). No. 19 is now demolished.

Princess Amelia (1711-1786) third daughter of George II, lived at No. 16 between 1761 and 1780, the house built by the Duke of Chandos. She gets a harsh press from her contemporaries: apparently horsey, crude and mischief-making. This house is much changed and is occupied on the Cavendish Square elevation by Coutts.

Lord Byron (1788-1824) was born around the corner in Holles Street – the site is now part of the John Lewis department store and a plaque commemorates him.

Queen Hortense (1783-1837) and her son Prince Charles Louis Napoleon (1808-73) resided in Holles Street in 1831. He was afterwards the last Emperor of France from 1852 to 1870.

Dr Joseph T Clover (1825-1882) a pioneer of anaesthesia, lived in the house which is now No.3 Cavendish Place between 1853 and 1882.

ST PETER'S, VERE STREET – THE OXFORD CHAPEL

On the south-west corner of the Estate stands St Peter's in Vere Street built as a chapel for the Earl of Oxford in 1724 on the western edge of the developing area: beyond lay open country. James Gibbs, who lived in Henrietta Street (now Place), was one of the Harley inner circle. He designed the Chapel and the Oxford Market. In the 19th century Edward Burne-Jones (1833-1898) designed the altarpiece as well as some of the stained-glass windows. The Chapel is now the headquarters of the London Institute for Contemporary Christianity.

The Portlands continued the northward expansion of the Estate, including Harley Street, Portland Place and Wimpole Street. The delayed development of Cavendish Square demonstrated that reliance on one's friends, however rich, was not without its drawbacks: completion was dependent on the fortunes and whims of men who might have other priorities, as indeed proved to be the case.

19. The church of St Peter in Vere Street.

20. Foley House.

FOLEY HOUSE AND THE VIEW NORTH

Thomas Foley, 2nd Baron Foley, was Edward Harley's first cousin. The Harleys and the Foleys were both ancient landed Herefordshire families. In 1753, Baron Foley, a bachelor, applied for a building lease on his cousin's estate just east of Chandos House. Chandos House, which never had a garden, only a mews and courtyard, would have overloooked the large garden of Foley House.

The widowed Countess of Oxford granted Foley a lease for 96 years and he thereby acquired the whole block just to the north-east of Cavendish Square on which to build a house with a garden looking north. Foley's plans contravened those of John Prince in 1719 and prevented the construction of a road running north and south through the middle of the Estate. Foley built a vast house and further petitioned the Countess of Oxford not to grant building leases north of his property, obstructing his view.

The Countess agreed this on 10 July 1758, but the formal documents implementing it were not signed at the last moment. A long and elaborate dispute resulted which was only finally settled on 30 January 1768, between William the 3rd Duke of Portland and Thomas Foley and which was then enacted by a private Act of Parliament confirming the provisions of the settlement and which indeed provided that the view north of Foley House would not be obstructed. As we shall see this pertains today and is the reason that Portland Place is so very wide and the view north is unobstructed.

In the 1770s, John Elwes (1714-1789), a property owner in Marylebone, helped to finance an ambitious project to the north-east of Cavendish Square, which was to be Portland Place. In 1773, Robert Adam hoped to make it a "street of palaces". This did not happen, but the brothers did acquire a number of plots and the interiors of some of the houses have characteristic ceilings and fireplaces. The street is the same width as Foley House then was, 125 feet.

In the event, Foley House was demolished in

21. *Portland Place in 1800.*

about 1812 to make way for Langham Place, the connecting link between Portland Place and the continuance of Regent Street – the grand route to the Regent's Park.

Nash sold part of the land he had acquired to the Crown and part to Sir James Langham on the understanding that Langham would hire Nash to construct Sir James's new town house. However, they had a dispute, partly due to the siting of the house, and partly because Sir James accused Nash of being a jerry builder since the house showed signs of structural faults. Also, the rear elevations of houses to be erected on Regent Street would be unacceptably close to Langham House. In the end, Nash amended the plans so that Langham Place curves around to meet Regent Street in the south and Portland Place on the north.

Langham House was later purchased by the Langham Hotel Company (*see p. 63*).

Elwes did not live to see the completion of his project, but he had been responsible for building a significant part of Georgian London. In addition to Portland Place, he had been responsible for parts of Oxford Circus, Piccadilly and Baker Street. He was believed to have been the inspiration for Charles Dickens's character Scrooge. He lived frugally, dressing in worn clothes, scrimping and saving. Having lived on only fifty pounds a year, he left half a million pounds to his sons.

NOTABLE RESIDENTS OF PORTLAND PLACE

An early resident of Portland Place was James Holroyd, the 1st Earl of Sheffield. A Whig, he owed his earldom to his efforts in bringing about the legislative union of England and Ireland in 1801. He was present in the House of Commons in June 1780, during the Gordon Riots. An angry mob tried to seize the Chamber. Allegedly Holroyd grabbed Gordon, told him that he was an absolute rotter, threatening him with physical violence. Gordon escaped when the mob surged off.

By the 1830s and 1840s, the social status of the inhabitants of Portland Place had declined. New residents comprised merchants, entrepreneurs,

22. *Devonshire Place, c. 1800.*

speculators, industrialists and bankers. The patrician residents had mostly moved on. Portland Place was nevertheless still an address conferring status, but its changing nature was indicated when a number of embassies were established there.

Daniel O'Connell (1775-1847), lived in Langham Place in 1836 when MP for Kilkenny. He had a serious difference of opinion with Benjamin Disraeli, and the latter challenged him to a duel for an insult. O'Connell had previously killed a man in a duel and had sworn not to engage in duelling again. The Irishman ignored the challenge but Disraeli, the initiator, was arrested and bound over to keep the peace.

[1] Richard Bowden, 'Buildings, Books, Debts and Drink' in *Westminster History Review*, 3, (1999).

[2] Information from Richard Bowden, archivist, The Howard de Walden Estate.

[3] John Summerson, *Georgian London* (1962), 82.

[4] A society of noblemen founded as a London dining club in 1734; they sponsored the study of ancient Greek and Roman art. Among their members were Joshua Reynolds and David Garrick.

[5] Quotation from his speech on the Reform Bill. Macaulay went on to note that Marylebone was without representation in Parliament.

[6] The Market, an essential amenity for the success of the Estate, cost over £6,000; its opening was delayed due to a dispute with the commercial interest of Lord Craven in Carnaby Street nearby; Bowden, *op cit.*

[7] Bowden, *op cit.*

[8] Oliver Bradbury 'Capital &Elegant', *Marylebone Journal* (Autumn 2005).

[9] Bowden, *op cit.*

A Change of Style

Not everyone rejoiced in the look created by the serried ranks of houses in the Palladian style emphasised by the architects in the circle of the Earls of Oxford and Mortimer (and from 1755 the Dukes of Portland) between 1717 to 1808, pre-eminently, Nash, Wyatt, the brothers Robert and James Adam, Bridgeman and Gibbs.

Sir Frank Marshall Elgood (1865-1948), felt that the imported Palladianism of Lord Burlington (and his ilk) had sapped English architecture of its native vigorous character. He wrote of what was then the new architecture in 1898:

> "it is only natural that architects should hark back to the time when architecture in England was on the progressive wane and attempt to start afresh from the point when inventive genius gave place to mere copyism. The possibilities of the style seem infinite … the effect is generally quiet and pleasing, has a thoroughly English appearance and is entirely suited to modern requirements. But this is not imitation of a past style. There is a wonderful originality in such designs and an entire absence of similarity or copying and who can say that it may not lead to what must be the desire of us all namely the formulating of a truly English twentieth century progressive architecture."[1]

Earlier, Disraeli wrote:

St Pancras is like Marylebone, Marylebone is like Paddington; all the streets resemble each other … Marylebone alone ought to have produced a revolution in our domestic architecture. It did nothing. It was built by Act of Parliament. It is Parliament to whom we are indebted for our Gloucester Places, and Baker Streets, and Harley Streets, and Wimpole Streets, and all those flat, dull, spiritless streets, resembling each other like a large family of plain children, with Portland Place and Portman Square for their respectable parent.

This was in contrast to Thackeray's description of Marylebone as the 'most respectable district of the habitable globe'. It also contrasts with our modern appreciation of the restrained symmetry of terraces of flat fronted terraced houses of brick or half stucco or Portland stone.

The views expressed by Elgood are anticipated by Sir George Gilbert Scott in 1858, who wrote in his *Remarks on Secular and Domestic Architecture*

> "the fact that in most of [London's] streets, such as Oxford Street, each man has built his house as he liked and that the whole is cut into vertical strips … is the one thing which redeems them from that abject insipidity which we see in … Harley Street. If everyone had a beautiful design of its own, differing in height in outline and in treatment and terminating in a good skyline our streets would at once become as pleasing as those of the great mediaeval cities."

THE ARTS AND CRAFTS MOVEMENT

Wimpole, Harley and Wigmore Streets have many individual houses which have been entirely rebuilt, frequently in an English Arts and Crafts or revival Queen Anne style. Pre-eminently, these were designed by A. Beresford Pite (1861-1934), C.H. Worley and R.J. Worley (separately) and Sir Frank M. Elgood (1865-1948), the latter having been the surveyor for the Howard de Walden Estate. Elgood designed at least nineteen houses in and around Wigmore, Wimpole and Harley Streets. His work deserves to be better known.[2]

Some of the work of these architects is shown in the big commercial buildings in Oxford Street. On the Howard de Walden Estate, we have chosen some addresses as examples, but there are many more. The reader is urged to walk these streets and observe the elements of this period of architecture amidst the remaining Georgian houses. [3 and 4]

Most of the original houses in Harley Street [5] and Wimpole Street were built in or about 1770. The 99-year leases therefore began to fall in about 1870. By then, styles had changed and an original house might have needed substantial repair or even re-building.

No 7 Harley Street (formerly no 86, built in 1756) was rebuilt in 1896 by R.J. Worley. The developer was J.S. Beale who was granted

23. *Wimpole House at 28-29a Wimpole Street, built by C H Worley in 1893.*

permission to demolish the original house and build residential flats of 'superior character'. The lease of 7 Harley Street was added to this development. Cherry and Pevsner describe the building as "overpowering terracotta", but this is grumpy: the building is powerful, arcaded with small paned leaded windows, which (as intended) catch the light. The building viewed from Cavendish Square manages exoticism. R.J. Worley also designed no. 3 Soho Square in a distinctive bow-fronted Arts and Crafts style with elegant Macintosh-type tree of life motifs.

No 37 Harley Street is unmissable. Designed in 1893 by A. Beresford Pite, with sculpture by F.E.E. Schenk, it is faced in Portland stone, the windows on the corner angled at 45 degrees from the east and south façades; the deep carving and human figures, reveal his interest in powerful decoration of sculptural importance. Pite also designed the West Islington Carnegie public library in Thornhill Square, Islington and as well in Foley Street All Souls school (1906-1908). He was also responsible for the façade of

Pagani's Restaurant at 42 Great Portland Street (1903),[6] sadly, destroyed in the last war, and 126 Great Portland Street.

No. 7 Wimpole Street is by Frank Elgood.[7] It is distinguished by the high ratio of fenestration to walling. This distinctive characteristic reminds one of buildings in Amsterdam.[8] The proportions of the storeys and the diminishing pilasters reflect Florentine private hotels; a balcony runs unbroken the width of the piano nobile. The very large windows with leaded glass and the surface decoration carved around the window frames are distinctive, different from the pre-occupations of other designs by Elgood. The design is very successful, albeit with some anomalies including the door case.

Records of the Howard de Walden Estate reveal that the original house at no. 7 Wimpole Street was demolished in 1911 and new construction was completed by 1913. In 1934, a lease for 999 years was acquired by John Everidge FRCS, which required him to allow the continued licences or renewals of licences to various

24. No. 81 Wimpole Street, built by Frank Elgood.

medical practitioners in the building.

Elgood, whose offices were at 98 Wimpole Street, rebuilt or refaced many town houses in this area including 81 Wimpole Street (1891), 39 Harley Street (1893-94), 49 and 51 Harley Street, 11 Welbeck Street (1905) and 32 Weymouth Street (1911). He also designed 6, 8 and 10 Wigmore Street, 45 and 47 Wigmore Street, 11 Great Castle Street, 5 Margaret Street, as well 73-75 Marylebone High Street.[9]

Wimpole House was 28, 29 and 29A Wimpole Street and the south side of New Cavendish Street. Four houses were demolished to rebuild on this site. It was designed by C.H. Worley and is entirely in terracotta in a renaissance decoration. It was built as a nursing home[10] in 1892 by Lithgow and Pappa. The corner stone, in distinctive art nouveau typeface moulded in the terracotta, states that it was laid by Mary Mason Lithgow. The building, with its distinctive roofline, makes an interesting mass on the corner.

C.H. and R.J. Worley designed number 41 Harley Street (1892). C.H. Worley also designed the Crown Hotel later known as Crocker's Folly *(see p 76)*. Later his style became both simpler and more elegant, but No. 41 is is a notable example of his early work, which is included in the list of buildings appended to an application to RIBA.[11]

[1] This quotation appears in Alastair Service *London 1900* (1979), 58.

[2] We are grateful to Alastair Service and Robert Thorne (mentioned in the footnote of Mr. Service's work, *London 1900* for their notable work on this architect.

[3] Cherry and Pevsner in *Buildings of England London 3: North West* (rev. edn 1999) is an accurate, if terse, guide. Alastair Service's *London 1900 (op. cit)* gives architectural description and photographs with eloquent commentary on social history; A.S. Gray's *Edwardian Architecture* (1985)provides description, photographs and a glossary of the architects.

[4] We are grateful for the time and research of Richard Bowden, archivist of the Howard de Walden Estate Office, who provided and explained the relevant material.

[5] Harley Street was definitively renumbered in 1866 when Upper Harley Street was included. There had been two prior renumberings.

[6] Service, *op. cit.* 143.

[7] We are indebted to Richard Bowden for contacting the holders of the lease for the information that the house was designed by Elgood.

[8] Oliver Bradbury kindly assisted in the description of this unusual house.

[9] Cherry and Pevsner, *op. cit*, 657.

[10] Information ex Richard Bowden.

[11] Information ex Oliver Bradbury.

The Portman Estate

The owners of the land of Marylebone wanted to follow the success of the development of Mayfair in which first Hanover, then Berkeley and finally the grand six acres of Grosvenor Square had been built, until the Reverend Sydney Smith could write, "I believe the [area] encloses more intelligence and human ability to say nothing of wealth and beauty than the world has ever collected in such a space before." Time was ripe for more development north of Oxford Street.

In 1755, nearly forty years after the early start of Cavendish Square, plans for the building of Portman Square between Gloucester Place and Baker Street were drawn up and it became the focus for development of land owned by the Portman Estate.

Sir William Portman (1497/8-1557), Lord Chief Justice of England, acquired the Portman Estate in the mid-sixteenth century. The Portmans also owned country estates in Dorset and Somerset. The initiative for building the Square came from a descendant, Henry William Portman in 1755, whose vision was to develop over 200 acres of meadow into a grand residential area. He took personal control over development from the design of buildings to their use. After Portman Square, the building of nearby squares followed: Manchester around 1770, Montagu in 1811 and Bryanston in 1824.

Portman Square was developed between 1764 to 1784. The most prominent residence is Home House at No. 20 at the north-west end. This was commenced by James Wyatt in 1772 and completed by Robert Adam in 1775. The house was intended as a palace of entertainment for Elizabeth, the Countess of Home. Its portico of Portland stone is distinguished by the Adam signature in the form of delicately articulated rams' skulls. This vast mansion of yellow London stock is decorated by raised Coade Stone roundels.

The Countess (1704-1784) was the daughter and heiress of a Jamaican sugar plantation and slave owner, William Gibbons, whose estate was known as Withywood, in the south-east of the island. Elizabeth was born in Jamaica and married at 16, in 1720, to James Lawes, who died in 1733. After his death, she moved to England

25. The north side of Portman Square, No. 56 of Ackerman's Repository of Arts, published in 1813.

26. *Home House, No. 20 Portman Square, early 20th century.*

27. *A ceiling decoration at Home House, 20 Portman Square.*

and, after nine years of widowhood, married William, the 8th Earl of Home, in 1742. On her death in 1784, Elizabeth left Home House and her substantial Gibbons estates in Jamaica "with negro and other slaves" in trust to her relation William Gale, who was resident in Jamaica.

There has always been a question as to why, when she already had a home on the south side of Portman Square, the Countess, long separated from her husband and at the age of 69, should have built a vast, even palatial, residence in the same square. Lesley Lewis,[1] asserts that there is, without too much speculation, a ready explanation: Elizabeth, without children, separated from her husband, may have embarked on this project to support and entertain her young kinswoman, Anne Horton (née Luttrell), a granddaughter of Elizabeth's first father-in-law, Nicholas Lawes, governor of Jamaica and also a plantation and slave owner.

Anne was a widow whose only child had also died. She caught the eye of Henry Frederick, Duke of Cumberland, a brother of George III, a dissipated, charming and musical man, given to falling in love and disappearing. In this case, the Luttrell clan insisted on marriage, the Duke agreed and they were married at her house in Mayfair. George III, when he learned of it, was incensed: his anger resulted in the Royal Marriages Act of 1772.

The king's opprobrium meant that the Duke (and his new Duchess) were shunned by society, but Elizabeth, Countess of Home, with her great personal wealth and her circle of friends, was able to be of help to Anne in hosting salons at her new house in Portman Square. In building this she may also have wished to use her talent in decorative matters[2] and perhaps the building project enthralled her. In short, Elizabeth had reasons to use her energy and money.

Elizabeth maintained a social circle of ex-patriot and visiting Jamaican planters which included William Beckford, author of *Vathek*, himself a rich absentee plantation owner, who wrote disrespectfully– and perhaps not entirely accurately– of the Countess. She was according to him, unconventional in her invitation to black musicians to perform in her own orchestra. Her music master complained that these gentlemen improvised, but she insisted.

The industrialist and art connoisseur, Samuel Courtauld (1876-1947), who lived in the house between 1927 and 1931, established the Courtauld Institute of Art in 1932, which used the house as its headquarters before moving to Somerset House in 1989. Between 1947 and 1974 Anthony Blunt (1907-1983) was Director of the Courtauld and Keeper of the Royal Family's pictures and drawings and a distinguished writer on architecture and art. He fell from grace when he confessed in 1964 to spying for the Russians but no public statement was made about this until 1979.

Home House was converted to a private members' club in 1996 and substantial sums spent on its restoration.

No. 21 was built for William Locke and extensively altered after 1866 when the entrance was moved to Gloucester Place. The interior was redesigned in 1972 for the Heinz Gallery and the RIBA Drawings Collection.

PLANTATION PEOPLE

From 1760 to 1780,[3] many planters, having made their money from sugar and other goods produced by slave labour[4] in the colonies, came to London as the profitability of sugar declined, by reason of an increase in the cost of buying human beings and the reduction in the price of sugar. Home House became a focal point for these returning expatriates, many of whose children had been born and raised in the West Indies. The coterie included Admiral Lord George Rodney (1719-1792), an opponent of the abolition of slavery, who had charge of the Naval Station of Jamaica. William Beckford jnr (1760-1844) was, as we have seen, a visitor.

Jane Austen alluded to these connections in *Mansfield Park* (1814*).* In the novel, Sir Thomas Bertram has interests in the West Indies. He departs to attend to these affairs and there is reference to the sorts of hazards which these kinds of travels entailed. When Sir Bertram's eldest daughter Maria becomes engaged to marry Mr Rushworth, they take a house in Wimpole Street (formerly belonging to a Lady Lascelles[5]) described in the novel as preferable 'to almost any... in London.'

Edward Moulton-Barrett, the father of Elizabeth Barrett (Browning) was rich from the proceeds of plantation ownership in Jamaica, and able to live in London, first at 99 Portman Square and later (at the time of Elizabeth's marriage to Browning) at a house which was on the site of 50 Wimpole Street. Elizabeth's mother was descended from a family of similar commercial interests.[6]

ELIZABETH MONTAGU AND THE FIRST BLUE STOCKING

Elizabeth Montagu (1720-1800) commissioned James 'Athenian' Stuart (1713-1788) to design a house (built between 1777-1782) to sit at a forty five degree angle on a large site forming the north-west corner of Portman Square across Gloucester Place from Home House. Her husband had died two years previously.

Originally, Elizabeth resided in Hill Street, Mayfair, where her salon became celebrated. When she came to live in Portman Square she described it as the 'Montpelier of England', and said that she 'never enjoyed such health as since she came to live in it'.

The house warming at Montagu House was a breakfast which seven hundred people attended. However, card playing and strong drink were not part of the entertainment which was certainly different from the arrangements at Home House. One of the rooms at Montagu House was decorated in bird feathers of all sorts collected from friends whilst another was painted with jasmine, roses and cupids.

Born Elizabeth Robinson in York, in 1742, and well educated, she married Edward Montagu, grandson of the 2nd Earl of Sandwich. He was then fifty, 28 years her senior and an MP and coal-mine owner of great wealth.

Elizabeth had, from an early age, been a close friend of Margaret, the daughter of Edward Harley, who had married the 2nd Duke of Portland. Elizabeth Robinson was thus accustomed to the intellectual society of her friend's house in London. Later, she herself became a leading light in the literary world. James Boswell commenting in his *Life of Johnson* on the gatherings at Mrs Montagu's house that

28. *Montagu (later Portman) House c.1830, by T.H. Shepherd.*

'it was much the fashion for several ladies to have evening assemblies, where the fair sex might participate in conversation with literary and ingenious men animated by a desire to please.'

An eminent member of these evenings was Benjamin Stillingfleet (1702-1771) who wrote an early opera and also published the first English editions of works by the Swedish botanist Linnaeus. Stillingfleet, it was observed, wore blue worsted stockings on these evenings, since he could not afford black silk stockings. Such was the excellence of his conversation, that his absences from the evenings were felt so great a loss, that it was said, 'We can do nothing without the blue stockings!' Thus the term 'blue-stocking' was invented, though it is now used to describe a *woman* of intellectual interests.

While Elizabeth Montagu may have competed with Elizabeth Home in the grandness of their entertainments, they socialised in different circles. As we have seen, Elizabeth Home was at the centre of expatriate slave owners at a time when intellectual Londoners were enthusiastic for reforms to abolish slave ownership. Elizabeth Montagu,[7] on the other hand, attracted to her house people who were celebrated in the arts and sciences. She was also famous as a letter-writer and a patron of the arts as well being the first English woman to write a book-length study of Shakespeare's drama. Dr. Johnson commented patronisingly that 'She diffuses more knowledge than any woman I know, or indeed, almost any man.' Every May Day she gave a feast of roast beef and plum pudding on her lawn to any chimney sweep or climbing boy who presented himself. A writer in *Cassell's Magazine*, May 1873, commented:

It is not generally known that this celebration

took its rise in a case of kidnapping which occurred — not to one of her children, for she never had any,[8] but to some member of her own or of her husband's family. It is said that the boy whose restoration she thus commemorated was stolen by chimney-sweeps when only three or four years old, and was brought back unintentionally to the house by some members of the sooty confraternity, when sent for to sweep the chimneys of her town mansion.

After her death in 1800 the Montagu family occupied the house until 1874 when the lease was taken by Lord Portman whose family members lived there until the house was destroyed by bombing in the Second World War. A hotel is now on its site.

A FASHIONABLE PLACE TO LIVE

The ambitions of William Henry Portman were realised when Portman Square became a desirable and fashionable place. James Boswell visited Portman Square in 1772 and remarked that the increase in London's fashionable quarters 'is prodigious'. Thackeray described the district as 'the elegant, the prosperous, the polite Tyburnia, the most respectable district of the habitable globe.' When he wrote *Vanity Fair* in the mid-1840s he placed Mrs. Hook Eagles 'a woman without a blemish in her character' in 'a house in Portman Square' to convey her place in society.

The artisans who worked in the houses for the rich lived in streets of more modest construction nearby such as New Quebec Street which consists today of flat-fronted houses of early Georgian design, almost all with later shop fronts.

Nearby, in Old Quebec Street, was Quebec Chapel, built for the Portman family in 1787 and named, rather belatedly, after General James Wolfe's victory in Canada in 1759. It was demolished to make way for the Church of the Annunciation (1912-1914), designed by Sir Walter Tapper.

To the west side of Portman Square is Gloucester Place which was built in 1810 by the same John Elwes of Portland Place. Wilkie Collins, who lived at No. 65, wrote *The Moonstone* there in 1867.

29. *Wilkie Collins, resident of Gloucester Place.*

30. *The Church of the Annunciation, on the site of the Quebec Chapel, 2007.*

No. 62 Gloucester Place was the home of Mary Anne Clarke, daughter of a bricklayer. Clarke kept ten horses, carriages, twenty servants and three cooks, a wealth derived from the fact that from 1802 to 1809, she was the mistress of Frederick, ('The Grand Old') Duke of York, one of George III's sons. The Duke gave Mrs.Clarke in 1802 the sum of £1,000 a year. In 1809, a scandal broke when the Duke faced the charge that he had promoted officers who had paid Clarke money – in return, presumably, for her influence with York. The Duke left Clarke and reduced her annual allowance to £400. She proved a match for this by threatening the publication of a memoir and extracted a pension from the government in return for not publishing. York resigned his position, although he was later reappointed, remaining in office until his death in 1827. In 1813, Anne Clarke was prosecuted for libel and subsequently imprisoned. On her release, she moved to France.

THE PONDS

There were many ponds in the area. They were apparently very deep and in the *St. James' Chronicle* of 8 August 1769 it was reported that "two young [sedan] chairmen were drowned. They had been beating a carpet in the Square and being warm and dirty had decided to have a bathe, not being aware of how deep the pond was."

MANCHESTER SQUARE

The principal building in the Square, Hertford House, which contains the Wallace Collection, (pp. 60-62) was leased by the Marquesses of Hertford.

Other residents of the Square have included John Hughlings Jackson (1835-1911), neurologist, who lived at No. 3, Julius Benedict (1804-1885), German-born composer, who lived at No. 2, and Alfred Lord Milner (1854-1925), British statesman and colonial administrator, at No. 14.

The eminent beauty, the former Sally Power, lived in Manchester Square briefly before she married Charles John Gardiner, Earl of Mountjoy, later 1st Earl of Blessington in 1818. Lady Blessington knew the 3rd Marquess of Hertford well and visited him in Paris. She found him amusing and original:

> "He has great natural talent and knowledge of the world, but uses them to little purpose save to laugh at its slaves … He is one of the many clever people spoilt by being born to a great fortune and high rank, advantages which exclude the necessity of exercising the talents he possesses."[9]

At nearby 7 Bentinck Street (the other side of Thayer Street), Edward Gibbon (1737-1794), the historian, rented a bachelor apartment and began the writing of *Decline and Fall of the Roman Empire*. He was there from 1773 to 1783. His comment on his residence gives insight into the pleasures of the area and of London in general:

> "I had now attained the solid comforts of life, a convenient well furnished house, a domestic table, half a dozen chosen servants, my own carriage, and all those decent luxuries whose value is the more sensibly felt the longer they are enjoyed … To a lover of books the shops and the sales in London present irresistible temptations … By my own choice I passed in town the greatest part of the year.[10]

AN EARLY ASIAN RESTAURANT IN LONDON

Lord Macaulay in his *History of England* considered the coffee house one of the "chief organs through which the public opinion of the metropolis vented itself."

No 34 George Street is the site of the first Asian restaurant in London – it was also a coffee house, which offered authentic Asian dishes. The Hindostanee was opened by Sake Dean Mahomet, a former officer in the East India Company Bengal Army, to cater for London's many Anglo-Indians. Mahomet wrote a book in 1794, *The Travels of Dean Mahomet*. He came to London in 1808, before opening his coffee house in 1810, serving Indian cuisine. The bamboo-cane sofas, chairs and paintings including Indian landscapes evoked an exotic ambience. In a separate smoking room, customers could inhale the smoke of tobacco blended and flavoured with herbs using the water-cooling system of hookah.

His advertisement in *The Times* read:

Hɪɴᴅᴏsᴛᴀɴᴇᴇ Cᴏꜰꜰᴇᴇ Hᴏᴜsᴇ, No. 34 George Street, Portman Square -East- Indian, informs the nobility and gentry, he has fitted up the above house … for the entertainment of Indian gentlemen, where they may enjoy the hookha, with real chilm tobacco, and Indian dishes, in the highest perfection, and allowed by the greatest epicures to be unequalled to any curries ever made in England with choice wines, and every accommodation …

In 1814 he left for Brighton, one of the pleasure grounds of the Prince of Wales, where he owned a therapeutic bathhouse. He wrote a manual on the art of shampooing and was appointed 'Shampooing Surgeon' to both George IV and his brother, the Duke of Clarence, the later William IV.

ECCENTRICS AND PROPHETS

Joanna Southcott (1750-1814), a self-appointed religious prophetess whose 'revelations' attracted many followers died in 1814 while living in Manchester Street, to the north of Manchester Square. The Southcottian movement survives in various forms today, including the House of David in America, and the Panacea Society of Bedford, England.

Another such was Richard Brothers (1757-1824) who lived in Upper Baker Street. Southcott cautioned her followers against him. His prophecy of the imminent death of George III (whose health, both physical and mental, was a politically sensitive matter) led to Brothers' arrest for treason in 1795. He died in 1824 and was buried in St. John's Wood Cemetery.

MONTAGU AND BRYANSTON SQUARES

At the same time that John Nash launched his scheme to build Regent's Park, David Porter, an ex-chimney sweep, began to develop Montagu and Bryanston Squares west of Gloucester Place. Porter's timing was prescient. He named Montagu Square after Elizabeth Montagu in appreciation of her annual May Day feasts for chimney sweeps *(see p. 34)*.

David Porter was born in 1747, starting life as

31. *Joanna Southcott.*

a chimney sweep. Chimney sweeps were in great demand as it was estimated that London had more than a third of a million chimneys; the work was dangerous, extremely dirty and could only be performed by very young children, who frequently suffered horribly, even suffocating. Porter, together with Jonas Hanway (the son of a magistrate, after whom Hanway Place is named), formed a friendly society to promote the interest and credit of chimney sweeps and to make proposals to regulate the trade. He became a very successful sweep himself and had a trade bill that boasted he swept the chimneys of Princess Amelia, a daughter of George II who lived in Cavendish Square. From the proceeds of his business he began acquiring building leases on the Portman Estate.

He employed James Thompson Parkinson, adviser to the Portman as well as other London estates, as the architect to build two new squares. However, both developments attracted censorious criticism. One writer in the 1840s stated that, 'Montagu Square and Bryanston

Square are twin deformities,' whilst another critic in *Builder Magazine* said, 'They are mere oblong slips with houses built in dreary uniformity; they are fortunately out of the way, and few people see them.'

The houses were all built with a basement, ground and three upper floors. There is no overall unanimity because the houses were designed for the individual requirements of the leaseholders. For example the first five houses in the south-east corner of Montagu Square, numbers 1 to 5, have narrower front basement areas than the others. The three in the centre on both sides of the square are larger than the rest and flat-fronted in contrast to the remainder, most of which have bays up to and including the first floor. The design of the bays appears to be unique to Montagu Square.

The novelist Anthony Trollope lived at No. 39 between 1873 and 1880 and located many of his fictional characters in Marylebone such as Mr Slope from *Barchester Towers* whose church was in Baker Street.

East of Montagu Square lies Dorset Street, the home of Charles Babbage (1791-1871). Sometimes referred to as the father of computing, he was the inventor of a machine for calculating and printing mathematical tables. In 1815, he settled at No.5 Devonshire Street before moving to No.1 Dorset Street in 1829, where he lived until his death. Babbage loathed street music and noise. He calculated that his working power had been reduced by twenty five percent from the noise of street traffic and congestion. He campaigned for the passage of an Act of Parliament (known as Babbage's Act), aimed at reducing unlicensed street activity, which the Act identified as a nuisance. Some of his neighbours hired musicians to play outside his windows. Writing in a long pamphlet called *Street Nuisances* (1864), he described the persecution to which he had been subjected in his once peaceful Marylebone home:

> Many years before, I had purchased a house in a very quiet locality...[but] the neighbourhood became changed: coffee-shops, beer-shops, and lodging houses filled the adjacent small streets.

32. *Anthony Trollope, caricature by Spy in* Vanity Fair, *in 1873. It was disliked by the author.*

> The character of the new population may be inferred from the taste they exhibit for the noisiest and most discordant music."

Running east-west and south of Dorset Street is Blandford Street where Michael Faraday (1791-1867), one of the 19th century's greatest scientists, credited with the discovery of electricity and conductivity, was himself discovered. Faraday was apprenticed to George Riebau, a bookseller, in Blandford Street for seven years from 1804. During his apprenticeship Faraday developed his interest in chemistry. In 1812, Faraday was given, by one of Riebau's customers, William Dance (1755-1840) (one of the founders of the Royal Philharmonic Society),

33. Michael Faraday.

four tickets to hear Humphrey Davy's lectures at the Royal Institution of Great Britain. Later that year Faraday applied to Davy asking for a position. At a second interview Davy appointed Faraday Chemical Assistant at the Royal Institution on 1 March 1813.

Bryanston Square, a long narrow north-south rectangle is, nevertheless, wider than Montagu Square. Among its residents have been the Duke of Brunswick (1804-1873) and of a different ilk, the artist Sir John Everett Millais (1829-1896). Appropriately, the Square was the address of Mr March in C.P. Snow's *The Conscience of the Rich* (1958).

STEPHEN WARD AND THE PROFUMO AFFAIR

Stephen Ward (1912-63), a socially well connected osteopath, lived at various times in a flat at Bryanston Mews West. He introduced Mandy Rice-Davies and Christine Keeler to a social set at Cliveden and Christine famously became both the lover of John Profumo, Secretary of State for War, and of Eugene Ivanov, a naval

34. The bookseller's in Blandford Street where Michael Faraday worked as an apprentice.

attaché at the Soviet Embassy. When it was all revealed Profumo resigned. Ward was charged with living off immoral earnings, and he committed suicide on the last day of his trial. Keeler was imprisoned on related charges, though Rice-Davies escaped prosecution. The Conservative government lost the election the following year.

DORSET SQUARE

The diminutive Dorset Square to the north of Marylebone Road was constructed between 1814 and 1822, and was the last of Marylebone's squares to be built. Three years before building commenced Dorset Fields had been the home of the Marylebone Cricket Club. In 1787, Thomas Lord, a bowler and groundsman with the White Conduit cricket club in Islington, was

35. Entrance to Thomas Lord's first cricket ground, in Dorset Square.

encouraged by Lord Winchilsea to lease a ground on Dorset Fields, owned by the Duke of Dorset, also a patron of the game. In that same year the Marylebone Cricket Club, which governed or influenced English cricket in some way until 1993, was formed. Lord's lease expired in 1810 and after a short stay at Marylebone Bank, Regent's Park, his cricket ground moved to a new site in St John's Wood in 1814, the present home of the MCC.

In 1802, a balloon ascent was made from Dorset Fields by André Ganerin whose craft covered a distance of six miles. Such was the interest that the Prince of Wales attended; one of the crowd was killed when a stand collapsed.

Dorset Square was never as fashionable as the squares to the south. Its architect James Thompson Parkinson planned a square surrounded by modest houses. Some of the original buildings survive on the north side, consistent with other Georgian building in Marylebone. During the Second World War No. 1 Dorset Square became the home of a branch of the Special Operations Executive (SOE). The SOE, sometimes referred to as 'the Baker Street Irregulars' after a fictional group of spies in a Sherlock Holmes novel, was initiated in July 1940 to conduct, encourage and facilitate espionage and sabotage behind enemy lines. It was also known as 'Churchill's Secret Army' and charged by him to 'set Europe ablaze'.

Sir Laurence Gomme (1853-1916) lived at No. 24 Dorset Square between 1895 and 1909. He pioneered the scheme to commemorate noteworthy London residents with blue plaques; he was also a campaigner for the protection of threatened buildings and in 1911 a founder of the London Museum. He contributed enormously to the history of London through his writings as well as his involvement with the formation of the *Survey of London* (now part of English Heritage's Research Department), and in jointly editing the *Victoria County History* series. *The Times* wrote that 'few men have had a more profound knowledge of the past and the present greatness of London, and few have done more to make London known to its people than Sir Laurence Gomme.'

Among those who also lived in Dorset Square was George Grossmith (1847-1912), writer, actor, and singer. He also worked with Gilbert and Sullivan, but was probably best known for co-authoring with his brother Weedon, the delightful and gently satirical novel, *Diary of a Nobody* (1892). Dorothy Gladys 'Dodie' Smith (1896-1990), novelist and playwright, best remembered for *One Hundred and One Dalmatians*, lived at No.19.

[1] Lesley Lewis, 'Elizabeth Countess of Home', *Burlington Magazine*, August 1967. Much of the material in this section on the Countess is based on the article.

[2] She commissioned two important memorials, one to her mother and one to her husband by John Cheere the only two of his works to be in Jamaica. They are among Jamaica's national treasures.

[3] The campaign against slavery developed in the late 1750s. The Slave Rebellion in Jamaica in 1760 led Quakers to ban their members from trading there; in 1778 The House of Commons set up a committee to investigate the slave trade; in 1787 the Society for the Abolition of the Slave Trade was formed. Influential figures such as John Wesley and Josiah Wedgwood gave their support. Later, they persuaded William Wilberforce to be their spokesman in the House of Commons.

[4] Peter Thorold in *The London Rich* (1999), stresses the connection between Marylebone and the West Indies. From a list of at least twelve residents of Portman Square, seven owned plantations. 'Both the principal Marylebone landlords acquired West Indian connections [loose term]:Edward Berkeley Portman marries Lady Emma Lascelles; and the Howard de Waldens, are descended from the Ellises and Palmers, both important Jamaican families... Edward Moulton-Barrett, father of Elizabeth Barrett Browning, was a member of the most important slave-owning families in the Caribbean.' (pp142-145)

[5] *Mansfield Park*: ch 40 'Then she will be in beauty, for she will open one of the best houses in Wimpole Street. I was in it two years ago, when it was Lady Lascelles's ...'

[6] Robert Browning's family were from St. Kitts; there is speculation that not only was Elizabeth Barrett Browning's father partly of black heritage, but Robert Browning was as well.

[7] In an article on Montagu, Bridget Hill 'The Course of the Marriage of Elizabeth Montagu: An Ambitious and Talented Woman without Means', *Journal of Family History*, Vol. 26, No. 1, (2001) 3-17, she states that 'Behind her growing restlessness and frustration, there lie aspects of her character–her obsession with money, her urgent need to be constantly admired and lauded, and her need to be in control of both people and things.'

[8] This is not accurate; she did have a child John, who died in 1744, while an infant. She did not have further children.

[9] Donald Mallett, *The Greatest Collector, Lord Hertford and the Founding of the Wallace Collection* (1979), 30

[10] G. A. Bonnard ed., *Edward Gibbon: Memoirs of My Life*, (1966), 183

Regent's Park

A PARK IN MARYLEBONE

Henry VIII 'acquired' what would become Regent's Park in the late 1530s to enlarge his hunting grounds near to central London. His new prize covered over 400 acres and was almost circular, as it is today. The Marylebone manor house *(see p.10)* and the home farm were used as accommodation for the Keeper of the Park. We don't know when the boundaries were determined, but Ann Saunders conjectures[1] that it may have been about 1539. A ring mound was thrown up around the boundary to keep the deer in and poachers out and lodges were erected for the gamekeepers. After Henry's death, his son, Edward VI, who also enjoyed hunting, made improvements. These included conduits bringing water to a number of brick-lined ponds for the deer.

However, Edward died young in 1553 and soon after, the new monarch, Mary I, granted the manor and manor house to Sir Henry Sydney to reward his loyalty during the short reign of Lady Jane Grey. Mary was not a great hunter and planned to sell off Marylebone Park for residential land, but this did not proceed. Elizabeth I, Mary's successor, did enjoy hunting there and made more improvements, so that the area could be used additionally for lavish entertainments. James I also relished the chase and ensured that Marylebone Park was well maintained. However, his successor, Charles I, eschewed hunting and, strapped for cash during the Civil War (1642-1646), in effect mortgaged the Park to two loyal supporters in return for military supplies. When it was surveyed for official purposes, the Park was found to contain 124 deer worth £130 and 16,297 trees. The property claims of the (dead) King's supporters found no favour with Cromwell after the War and he included Marylebone Park in a long list of royal possessions which he decided to sequestrate to offset the expenses of the Parliamentary forces. Large numbers of trees were cut down to provide building materials for naval vessels and the deer were removed. The largest parcel of land went to Colonel Thomas Harrison, one of the men who had signed the death warrant of Charles I.

At the Restoration in 1660, Charles II settled some scores: Harrison was executed as a regicide and his holdings in Marylebone Park and the lesser holdings of other supporters of Parliament were in turn sequestrated and the leases redistributed among Royalists. Hunting had already ceased in the Park and most of it was divided into parcels for farming. It made good soil for dairy farming and market gardening and hay was grown in the meadows. Londoners needed fresh dairy products and as they were dependent on horses for transport, supplies of hay were essential. The 19th-century historian Thomas Macaulay commented on the rural nature of Marylebone in the mid-1680s as a place where '*cattle fed and sportsmen wandered with dogs and guns…*'

But Marylebone was about to change. In 1789, Marylebone Park was surveyed by Thomas Marsh setting out all of the fields and boundaries and, usefully, depicting landmarks.

EARLY BUILDINGS IN MARYLEBONE PARK

The Queen's Head and Artichoke and another inn nearby called the Jew's Harp near the site of today's The Holme were popular places. There was a wheelwright's yard; and James Wyatt, RA rented a large carpentry and joinery workshop there, near his house at 69 Queen Anne Street East (now Queen Anne Street).

In a nearby group of buildings was the artificial stone manufactory of John Charles Felix Rossi. He lived in Lisson Grove, not fifteen minutes away. Rossi had worked at Coade's Artificial Stone Manufactory in Lambeth but in 1798 set himself up in the Park, remaining there until 1810. He received several commissions from his neighbour Wyatt. Rossi also made the angels for the cupola of the present Marylebone parish church, though probably not in this manufactory as the church dates from 1814.[2]

In 1803, a top-lit building designed by George Edwards, constructed near where Park Square

36. *The Jew's Harp and its tea gardens; watercolour c.1800, artist unknown.*

now stands, appeared as a temporary gallery to house the art collection of Joseph, Count Truchsess-Zeyl-Wurzach who was the Grand Dean of Strasbourg Cathedral. The Count had been forced to move his collection comprising works by German, Flemish, Italian and a few French artists from Wurzach to Vienna because of the Napoleonic wars. Later, in financial difficulties, he decided to exhibit the pictures for sale in London, hoping that the British government would buy it for the nation. The gallery provided a refreshment room and catalogue. The subscription for purchase was unsuccessful, however and the government declined the purchase. It was supposed that amongst the vast collection of 966 pictures by 635 artists, there were copies or fakes and word may have got around. Eventually the pictures were auctioned in three lots: the Count recouped his costs, but not his capital. He reserved the best pictures and eighty-one of these are in the Art Gallery and Museum at Darmstadt. The gallery was sold and dismantled in 1806.

AN EARLY GARDEN CITY

The Crown hunting ground was about to be transformed by a vast, bold and successful venture in town-planning which created the residences, villas, streets and park known as Regent's Park. The concept was the inspiration of a talented and well-connected civil servant,

John Fordyce (1735-1809), Surveyor-General of the Crown Estates, the architect, John Nash (1752-1835) and the Prince of Wales, by 1811 the Prince Regent, and later George IV.

The leases of most of the land were due to revert to the Crown in 1811 and Fordyce foresaw that the location of Marylebone Park on the edge of the expanding metropolis made development inevitable. The greatest financial benefit was at the rich, fashionable end of the market: the prior developments of the Bedfords and the Grosvenors and much later the Portlands and the Portmans proved this. The notion was to develop the Park as a planned residential quarter for London's elite while retaining part of it as a green space for the recreation of all Londoners. Additionally, there was to be a grand avenue joining the Park to the political and diplomatic centre of Westminster and leading to the Prince's Carlton House. Clearly a man of vision, Fordyce, however, died in 1809 and it was left to others to develop his ideas and put them into effect.

John Nash was an architect of genius, a man of bold vision, hard-headed in business matters, and a natural 'fixer'. He was a well-regarded and effective manager of those he employed and possessed good negotiating skills. He was nearly sixty and the official Architect and Surveyor of Woods and Forests (of the Crown Estates) when he began working on this enormous project. He already possessed an impressive record of designing houses for discerning clientele[3] and his contacts included extremely influential people, such as the Prince Regent. The Prince may have been a libertine, obsessed with satiating his sexual, aesthetic and culinary desires, but he was also a man of high culture, enthusiastic and knowledgeable about architecture. He was prepared to spend vast sums of (his own and other people's) money and for him the 3rd Marquess of Hertford (with whose second wife Isabella, the Prince was enthralled) and others bought artworks of quality in quantity.

In Nash, the Prince found a friend and kindred spirit, and a man eager to push back the boundaries of what was regarded as possible in architecture and to flout convention. The

37. The Park as developed at the beginning of the 20th century. The Baptist College in the north-west occupies Holford House, designed by Decimus Burton c. 1832. The building was destroyed in the last war. The map was compiled before the rude intrusion of the Bedford College buildings, which occurred in 1913, when it surrounded and then caused the demolition of South Villa (see Ill. 44).

outcome of this aspect of their relationship is seen in grand style in the exoticism of the Royal Pavilion at Brighton.

The challenge of the Park appealed to both men. Nash and the Prince envisaged not only the preservation and development of Marylebone Park but the creation of a distinctive and opulent residential enclave which would affect the future development of London and which would be unlike anywhere else: until Baron Haussman rebuilt Paris, it certainly was. The grand new wide road (Regent Street) would sweep from the Prince's extravagant mansion, Carlton House, south of Pall Mall, to their new prestige residential development in the Park, where the Prince was to have another 'palace' facing Cumberland Terrace (the palace was, in the event, not built). The intention was to rival or preferably exceed in dignity and grandeur the Rue de Rivoli being built to the orders of Napoleon Bonaparte in Paris. Regent Street was to cross Piccadilly and then, further north,

Oxford Street. Its route would involve the demolition of slum property on land which already belonged to the Crown and would separate the swanky area around Hanover Square from the more louche (and meaner) streets of Soho just to the east. The Park, quickly becoming known as Regent's Park,was to be a self-contained residential estate with limited road access and protected from working class areas close by. It would not be 'gated', but be 'separate' – enough to reassure the proposed residents. High class housing in villas, terraces and crescents would be built in spacious surroundings whose attractions were social exclusivity, closeness to the capital's amenities while set amidst the 'controlled' sylvan delights of a designed Park. Nash's plan of co-ordinated themed buildings, related in materials and design but distinct, with co-ordinated streets and planned open spaces, was an early version of a garden city.

The façades were to be stucco reflecting light and giving a sense of opulence. The scheme included a lake taking advantage of part of the course of the Tyburn stream *(see p. 8)* in the south-west of the Park and with the proposed Regent's Canal providing the northern boundary. On the other side of Albany Street on the east, was to be a quarter providing supplies and services for the Park's residents. Its existence is recalled today by the street name Cumberland Market. Beneath one part of this service area was an underground ice house, owned by a William Leftwich who brought his supplies of ice from Norway and had them delivered via the London Docks and the Regent's Canal. When the Cockfosters extension of the Piccadilly Line was built, spoil from that project was used to fill the cavern of the icehouse.

The great esteem in which the Prince Regent held Nash and the close relationship between them conferred power on Nash and enabled him to go where others could not. It also elicited jealousy. There were some who would have rejoiced if the project were a disaster. Nash's closeness to the Prince Regent was the subject of gossip.

The plans originally proposed by Nash were substantially modified by the Commissioners, for example, the Regent's Canal (opened from Paddington to Camden Town in 1816) was moved to the northern boundary and the 'Outer Circle' would form a complete perimeter, while the 'Inner Circle', as the name suggests was set inside and is perfectly round. Work on the grand project began in 1812. However, by 1816, Nash's estimates of costs were seriously exceeded and a host of problems were being encountered. In particular, the demand for residences proved unreliable, especially in the depression following the Napoleonic wars, and the new street connecting to Westminster was proceeding so slowly that the project evoked scorn. There were disputes with people whose property and other interests were affected by the scheme. Nash displayed fortitude and determination though under scrutiny from the Commissioners of the Crown Estate Office who were looking for returns on the investment. The Prince Regent, who in 1820 became King George IV, kept his nerve and supported Nash by commissioning the work on the design of the Brighton Pavilion and, from 1825, the rebuilding of Buckingham Palace.

Nash takes much of the credit for Regent's Park, even though the full plan was not built.

The earliest development was **Park Crescent** in the south-east corner and Cornwall Terrace (1821) was the first terrace to be built, designed by Decimus Burton with Nash's approval and built by the young Decimus's father, James Burton.

The South Side:
To the west of Park Crescent are the two York Terraces divided by York Gate which provides a vista to the parish church of St. Marylebone.

Moving clockwise around the outer circle, **Cornwall Terrace** is followed by **Clarence Terrace,** designed in 1823 by Decimus Burton.

Sussex Place, between **Clarence Terrace** and **Kent Terrace** (of 1827) built in 1822 stands out as a contrast to Nash's neo-classical terraces with its curved end wings and ten paired vast painted cupolas. There is, perhaps, a hint of the playfulness evident in the Royal Pavilion at

Brighton. Its façade is all there is left of the original: it has been entirely rebuilt as the London Business School.

Continuing, **Hanover Terrace** designed by Nash was built in 1822 and **Kent Terrace** (behind to the south) in 1827.

Close by **Hanover Lodge** is Sir Frederick Gibberd's London Central Mosque. The origin of this building, with its 140 ft minaret, goes back to the 2nd World War when many Muslim soldiers from the Indian subcontinent were in London.

To the north is the Zoo. Then the Outer Circle turns south past Gloucester Gate which was designed by Nash. The actual builder and his architect disagreed with the proportions so the builder enlarged the mouldings on the capitals without telling Nash.

From 1821, Nash was working on Regent Street and by 1827, he was busy with Buckingham Palace. He may have been unable to attend to the detail. Passing Gloucester Gate, he remarked that the mouldings looked larger than he expected and left it at that. Close by is St Katherine's Chapel of 1829. Formerly the chapel of St Katherine's Royal Hospital and now the church of the Danish community in London, this has a coffered ceiling. In a garden nearby, stands a replica of the 'Jelling Stone', a famous Runic monolith from Denmark.

The terraces of houses from the north-east corner of the Outer Circle down to Park Crescent comprise **Gloucester Gate**, **Cumberland Terrace**, and **Chester Place** and **Terrace** and **Cambridge Terrace** and **Cambridge Gate**. These were built from 1825 to 1827. To the east of Albany Street are **Park Village East** and **West**, two fanciful developments by Nash and his pupil and relative, James Pennethorne, erected in the 1820s and 1830s.

Cumberland Terrace (1826) was designed by Nash and is the most splendid of his terraces in the Park. It was intended to stand opposite the pleasure palace for the Prince but this was never built. The Terrace consists of three main blocks linked by decorative arches and it is dominated by a magnificent pediment adorned with a mass

38. *Chester Terrace on the eastern side of the Outer Circle. The dome of the Colosseum can be seen in the background.*

of statues intended to evoke the spirit of the Empire

Chester Terrace, also designed by Nash, was constructed by James Burton. Originally Nash had intended to place a statue on the top of each of the building's 52 Corinthian columns. He may have been something of a showman but eventually even he, casting a critical eye over the early ones to be built, decided that they looked ridiculous. No more were erected and those which had been built were taken down.

The large block of flats at Cambridge Gate built between 1876 to 1880 were built on the site of the Colosseum described on p. 127. The modern Royal College of Physicians, just where the Outer Circle turns west, was designed by Denys Lasdun in 1964. It replaced the Nash-designed Someries House.

The Junction with Marylebone Road

Park Crescent at the north end of Portland Place was originally planned by Nash as a full circus and intended to be a triumphal entry into the Park, but only the southern semi-circle was built. Construction started in 1812, but was not completed until 1818 because of the bankruptcy of the initial builder.

The layout of the roads, the original landscaping and the placing of the terraces and residences on the principal thoroughfares were those of Nash in conjunction with the Commissioners, but he was less able to influence

39. *The Holme, overlooking the lake, the first major building of the young Decimus Burton.*

the quality of the construction of individual buildings and their interiors. Despite specifications in the contracts, the grandness of the decorative façades was not matched by equivalent quality of the architectural detail, design, or finish of the interiors.

THE VILLAS

Not all of Nash's plans were realised for he had orginally envisaged building 56 villas in the Park. Only eight were built, of which only two survive. There were several individual villas built on the periphery (and outside) the Inner Circle. **St John's Lodge** was designed by John Raffield and exhibited in 1818 at the Royal Academy. **The Holme** (*c*.1818), which was the first commission for the 18-year-old Decimus Burton, trained by Nash, was built for his father, the builder, James Burton. This is picturesquely sited by the boating lake. The house became part of the campus of Bedford College but is now again a private residence. Finally, **South Villa** (1827) was also taken over by Bedford College but demolished when the current buildings on the site (now occupied by Regent's College) were designed by Basil Champneys.

St John's Lodge on rising ground close to the Inner Circle looks towards the Zoo and Primrose Hill. It was much altered in the mid-19th century. It was the residence of the Marquess of Wellesley,

Wellington's elder brother, Governor General of India, Foreign Secretary and finally Lord Lieutenant of Ireland. From 1842 to 1887 the house was held by Sir Francis Henry Goldsmid, the first Anglo-Jewish baronet. The Goldsmids were originally from Portugal and were bankers. Goldsmid was a prison reformer, philanthropist and educationist and an eloquent advocate of Jewish emancipation in this country. In 1889 the Lodge was acquired by the 3rd Marquess of Bute as his London residence and his family retained it until the 1st World War.

Two terraces running around the northern perimeter were never begun nor was Nash's scheme for a double circus (the inner circle) of residential buildings in the centre of the park.

In the west of the Park, the 3rd Marquess of Hertford, then Lord Yarmouth, commissioned Hertford Villa to be built by Decimus Burton in 1825. It was probably complete by 1831, and consisted of two classical buildings linked by the very grand and exotic Tent Room, intended for lavish entertainments and with balconies for the Marquess's special guests. When, in 1829, the Marquess bought the striking clock from the the church of St. Dunstan's-in-the-West, Fleet Street, which was being demolished and rebuilt, he installed it in his garden and renamed the house **St. Dunstan's Villa**. Inside, hung the imposing and characterful portrait of the 3rd Marquess of about 1825 by Sir Thomas Lawrence.[4] A later tenant, from 1914 to 1917, was the merchant banker, Otto Kahn of the house of Kahn Loeb. He surrendered the lease to a training institute for the blind, and the villa gave its name to that organisation founded by the publisher, Sir Arthur Pearson, for blinded soldiers and sailors. In the twenties, St. Dunstan's was empty, but in 1935 to 1936 it became briefly the home of Lord Rothermere who returned the clock to St. Dunstan's church. (The church, which had been rebuilt in 1832 and again, after bombing in 1944, re-opened in 1950). In 1936, the Villa was purchased by Barbara Hutton, the American heiress of Woolworth's. She demolished it in 1937, building Winfield House, now the home of the U.S. Ambassador in London.

40. *St. Dunstan's Villa on the western side of the park, now supplanted by Winfield House, the residence of the US Ambassador in London. The St Dunstan clock may be seen far left.*

THE PUBLIC AND THE PARK

Access for the public to Regent's Park was an issue. Nash had laid out the residential quarter as an integral part of the Park, but separate from it, and the Prince Regent always had in mind that the public should be able to make full use of the space. But early residents without private gardens campaigned for reserved gardens of the sort in many of London's fashionable squares for the exclusive use of the key-holders. For a period the area between Hanover Terrace, Sussex Place, Cornwall Terrace and the lake was fenced off for their benefit. It was claimed that this would help to protect young trees and also discourage the activities of those wishing to visit the park for nefarious purposes. However, the roads within the Park were open, and the later policy of the Royal Parks was to maximise the space available for the use of the general public. On the expiration of leases, more of the Park was made accessible as conditions of new leaseholds.

THE INNER CIRCLE

Within the Inner Circle are the pretty Queen Mary's Garden and the Open Air Theatre. The Royal Botanic Society laid out Gardens in 1838; a pioneering conservatory of iron and glass was built and annual flower shows became a feature. The Society closed the Gardens in 1932, because it could not afford increased rents. Queen Mary's Garden was developed in 1935. The area now includes the rose gardens, a cascade, a Japanese garden, the Begonia Gardens, the Triton Fountain, the Mediterranean and herbaceous borders and the Jubilee Gates of 1935. The Broad Walk comprises the restored formal gardens, with fountains, in the French manner. These contrast with the cultivated naturalism and artful wildness devised by Humphry Repton and his followers for English gardens of this period.

The Open Air Theatre was established in 1932, and has one of the largest theatrical auditoriums in the country.

NEW VILLAS

Clockwise from the Mosque along the Outer Circle and backing on to the canal are now six villas built between 1988 and 1990 to the designs of Quinlan Terry. Each of them evokes a different style, Palladian, Venetian, Gothic, Regency, Corinthian and Tuscan. Architecturally, they look to the past, but for some critics, the inability to design buildings in a modern style suitable for the location was disappointing.

NOTABLE RESIDENTS

At No. 23, Park Road lived **José de San Martin** (1778-1850). He played a leading part in the successful struggle of Argentina, Chile and Peru for independence from Spain.

Hanover Lodge, designed by Nash, is now a students' hall of residence but it was once the home of **Admiral Earl Beatty** (1871-1936), veteran of the First World War battles of the Dogger Bank and Jutland. An earlier resident was **Thomas Cochrane,** 10th Earl of Dundonald (1775-1860), successful as a frigate captain capturing enemy ships. Though officers and other ranks competed to be under his command, he made powerful enemies in a campaign against corruption in the navy; in 1814, he was charged with fraud and was discharged and imprisoned. He later sailed in the navies of Chile, Peru, Brazil and Greece. Eventually, he was pardoned and given flag rank in the Royal Navy. His exploits were the inspiration for some of the naval tales of C S Forester and Patrick O'Brian.

Wilkie Collins (1824-1889) was a resident at No. 2 Cornwall Terrace in 1859. *The Woman in White* and *The Moonstone*, his most famous works, were published in 1860 and 1868 respectively

Alfred Noyes (1880-1958), the poet, lived at 13 Hanover Terrace from 1929 to 1935 as did **H.G. Wells** (1866-1946) from 1937 until his death.

E H Shepard (1879–1976) the illustrator of A A Milne's Winnie the Pooh books as well as *Now We are Six* and *When we were very young* and, after the book (without illustrations) was already famous, *The Wind in the Willows* by Kenneth Grahame, spent his childhood in Kent Terrace. Shepard also worked for *Punch* for many years being sacked in 1953 at the age of 74.

Lord Lister (1827-1912) lived at No.12 Park Crescent. He was an early proponent of the techniques of antiseptic surgery, which did so much to increase the survival rates after invasive surgery. His pioneering work led to surgeons being able to undertake more complicated operations with far greater safety.

Sir Charles Wheatstone (1802-1875) lived at No.19 Park Crescent. He was a physicist and in 1837 in conjunction with William Cooke, he took out a patent for an electric telegraph, the fastest form of communication then known. It was quickly adopted by the major railway companies, improving the safety of their operations. He was also the inventor of the concertina.

THE ZOO

The Zoological Society of London was founded in 1826, mainly the inspiration of Sir Stamford Raffles (1781-1826) (who also founded Singapore), with the purpose of forming a collection of species that would be the basis for scientific research and public interest. The first architect and designer was Decimus Burton, whose buildings were handsome but entirely unsuitable for the creatures that occupied them. The Zoo opened to members in 1828, but not fully to the public until 1847. There were 30,000 visitors in the first seven months. In 1835 came the first chimpanzee, followed by four giraffes a year later; the world's first reptile house opened in 1843 and an aquarium followed ten years later. An insect house opened in 1881.

Improvements to the facilities and accommodation for the animals have been continuous and have resulted in an eclectic collection of buildings such as Lubetkin & Tecton's Penguin Pool of 1934 and the Elephant and Rhino Pavilion by Casson, Conder & Partners of 1965. The group of buildings, not always complementary or easy on the eye, are intended to serve the interests of the animals they house. Best-known of the modern buildings is perhaps the elegant, tensile aviary designed in 1964 by Price, Newby and Lord Snowdon.

During the Second World War, the Zoo remained open, but the poisonous snakes and insects were destroyed and the Aquarium drained. Many of the animals were evacuated to Whipsnade. In September 1940 a bomb fell in the zoo area. In the resulting pandemonium a zebra escaped pursued by the Society's eminent Secretary, Professor Julian Huxley.

41.   The Zoological Gardens c. 1830.

THE TOXOPHILITE SOCIETY

In 1832 the Toxophilite Society was allotted five acres close to York Terrace. After opposition from residents many joined the Society and the sport of archery became emblematic of polite recreation acceptable to young ladies prevented by convention from so many other forms of exercise. The Toxophilites continued to practise their skills on this site until they moved in 1922.

42.   Ladies' Day at the Toxophilite Society early 20th century.

SKATING ON THIN ICE

When the lake froze thousands of Londoners flocked to enjoy skating or to laugh at beginners. The Royal Humane Society, a voluntary body founded in 1774, established stations by London's rivers and lakes and 'Icemen' acted as lifesavers. On 15 January 1867, the Society posted notices warning of danger in Regent's Park. The condition of the ice deteriorated and as it broke up, skaters fell into the freezing water. Their heavy skates and clothing impeded their attempts to keep afloat or get to shore and the icemen were overwhelmed. Forty bodies were recovered.

The lake was drained and made shallower before the water was restored. In 1886, the same happened, but disaster was averted because the lake was shallow; there were no fatalities.

DETERIORATION AND THE SECOND WORLD WAR

The increasing commercialisation and density of the West End made the Park and the Park Villages desirable, but by 1931 the deepening economic depression meant that many grand homes in the Park stood empty with the

43. *The scene of the great ice disaster at Regent's Park lake in 1867, as depicted in the* Illustrated London News.

consequent deterioration of their fabric and appearance.

During the Second World War the Park and its buildings received substantial bomb damage and others suffered neglect because of austerity measures. Few were undamaged or structurally sound and some were derelict and at the end of the war decisions as to the Park's future became urgent. In the event a small amount of demolition and redevelopment took place, but much property was refurbished or completely rebuilt behind the old or replica façades. The then local authority's plan to demolish and replace the terraces with dense high-rise housing to alleviate the housing shortage was mercifully not implemented.

[1] Much of the detail in this section relies upon Ann Saunders, *Regent's Park from 1086 to the Present* (rev. edn 1981), the best and most comprehensive book on the subject.

[2] *Ibid*, 57.

[3] Cronkhill, near Shrewsbury, 1802; Caerhays Castle, Cornwall, 1808, Grovelands Park, Enfield, 1797 and later the Brighton Pavilion.

[4] Now in the National Gallery in Washington, DC.

44. *The Crown Commissioners in 1913 ignored the protests of public opinion and allowed the building of the eight blocks which made up Bedford College and necessitated the demolition of St John's Villa. Permission to build was given without the knowledge of Parliament. The complex is now the Regent's College. This drawing, by Harold Oakley, was published in* The Graphic *on 5 July 1913. The College was opened that day.*

Marylebone pleasures

MARYLEBONE GARDENS

Marylebone Gardens began in the latter half of the 17th century as not much more than bowling greens and gardens, reached through the grounds of the Rose of Normandy tavern in Marylebone High Street. Pepys visited them in this early guise in 1668, when he recorded in his diary 'Then we abroad to Marrowbone, and there walked in the garden: the first time I ever was there, and a pretty place it is'. The transformation to full pleasure gardens to compete with Vauxhall took place in 1738 when Daniel Gough, proprietor of the Rose, opened the Gardens for evening entertainment. When enlarged to their fullest extent in 1753 they encompassed eight acres, extending east about as far as present-day Harley Street and south to Weymouth Street. No.35 Marylebone High Street is on the site of the former entrance. The gardens lay behind the old manor house which was demolished in 1791 – the site of this is now occupied by a garage.

The new Gardens enjoyed the patronage of the rich and fashionable, if somewhat dissolute and raffish. A range of entertainments was available. There were theatrical performances, balls and concerts and magnificent firework displays. Dr Arne (1710-78), the composer of *Rule Britannia*, was musical director for a time and it became the practice to perform the works of Handel when they were published. The Reverend Dr. John Fountaine, headmaster of a school 'for young gentlemen' occupying the manor house for much of the 18th century, was friendly with Handel.

The still largely rural location of Marylebone Gardens meant that many patrons made their way across the open Marylebone fields, where highwaymen and thieves enjoyed easy pickings. As early as 1716, the *Evening Post* recorded: On Wednesday last four gentlemen were robbed and stripped in the fields between London and Marylebone. In *The Beggar's Opera*, first performed in 1728, the fictional highwayman, Captain Macheath, uses the area for his depredations.

In the 1750s, the owner of the Gardens was a Mr Trusler, whose daughter was renowned for the excellence of her catering. On 6 May 1759, the *Daily Advertiser* carried the following announcement:

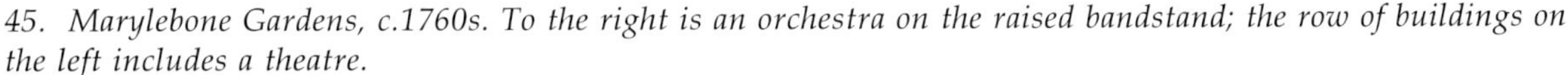

45. Marylebone Gardens, c.1760s. To the right is an orchestra on the raised bandstand; the row of buildings on the left includes a theatre.

Mr Trusler's daughter begs leave to inform the nobility and gentry, that she intends to make fruit-tarts during the fruit season; and hopes to give equal satisfaction as with the rich cakes and almond cheesecakes. The fruit will always be fresh gathered, having great quantities in the garden; and none but loaf sugar used, and the finest Epping butter. Tarts of a twelvepenny size will be made every day from one to three o'clock …

In 1774 the owner put on a fête champêtre, for which the entrance fee was five shillings. A second such event featured a firework display arranged by the French pyrotechnic artist, Monsieur Torré.

Marylebone Gardens contained an area known as 'The Bear Garden', featuring pits for cock-and dog-fighting. Spectators, their purse strings loosened by drink, bet huge sums on these contests. There were also rings for bare-knuckle boxing. Generally, the largest crowds were attracted by bouts between women.

The Gardens enjoyed a renaissance in the 1770s because of the 'Marylebone Spa'. A spring was found there in 1773, the water from which, it was claimed, aided digestion and was efficacious for those suffering from nervous, scorbutic and other disorders. A shilling was charged to drink the waters.

The end of Marylebone Gardens was not the result of any campaign to improve public morals and behaviour. Quite simply, Marylebone became engulfed by bricks and mortar. Land values rose and the site of the Gardens became valuable and they closed in 1778. The Marylebone Music Hall, built in 1856, stood on the site of the Rose of Normandy.

THE SHELL WORK GROTTO[1]

Grotto Passage is a pedestrian passage running south off Paddington Street and just to the east of Ashland Place. Its name reminds us of John Castles, a shell work artist. In his early days, he presented to King George III the Royal Arms executed in shell work and he also erected a grotto for Sir Robert Walpole at Chelsea. Castles leased a one and a half acre site of land on the west side of Marylebone High Street where he

erected sheds and tents for the display of his elaborate work. In 1737, he established a shell grotto which, fortuitously, was opposite the entrance to Marylebone Gardens. Thomas Smith, in his *Topographical and Historical account of the Parish of St. Mary-le-bone* (1833) wrote:

> Grotto Passage in Paradise Street, having been erected on the site of an Exhibition of Shell work called the Great Grotto; the ingenuity of this artist appears to have been duly appreciated by the Public his exhibition having been a celebrated place of fashionable resort.

John Castles was interred in the cemetery nearby with a stone commemorating 'John Castles late of the Great Grotto whose great ingenuity in shell work gained him universal applause'. Shell work was a popular hobby amongst the rich who could afford to buy large quantities of exotic specimens from ships returning to England laden with such items.

NEW PLEASURES

Marylebone High Street follows the route of the Tyburn *(see p. 8)*. After a long period of decline, there has been a renaissance of smaller shops of individual proprietorship mingled with a selection of more up market multiples.

The premises of Daunt Books are a notable example at Nos. 83-4. An advertisement in the 1950s' guidebook, *St. Marylebone Past and Present,* reveals that on the site from 1855 was Francis Edwards Ltd., bookseller at No. 83. Research by the current proprietor shows that the premises were redeveloped between 1910 and 1912 when the catwalk was built and the rear of the shop extended. Cherry and Pevsner confirm that the façade is early 20th century.

The advertisement indicates that the shop specialised in 'original editions and in particular travel' and out of print books. They also made valuations of libraries. The façade of No. 83 was copied and extended to No. 84, when Daunt Books took over the lease.

At No.35 Marylebone Lane is a small delicatessen, Paul Rothe & Son, at which four generations of the same family have operated. It was opened in 1900 by Paul Rothe, who had

FRANCIS EDWARDS
LIMITED
Booksellers in Marylebone since 1855

BOOKS ON ALL SUBJECTS:

Original Editions — Early Voyages and Travels, Africa, America, Asia, Australia, Atlases and Maps, Topography of Great Britain, Anthropology, Early Printed Books, Books in Fine Bindings, First Editions, Library Editions, Coloured Plate Books, etc., also Historical and Literary Manuscripts, Autograph Letters, etc.

"Out-of-Print" Books searched for free of charge

Valuations made for Probate, Insurance, etc.

Catalogues are issued at frequent intervals and will be sent post free on application

Hours of Business:
Monday—Friday 9.15-5.30.   *Saturday* 9.15-12.30

come to England from Germany. His son Robert was born in 1915 in the flat above the shop and he operated the business until he was 69. The business changed over the years, going into catering.

At No. 19, in a two-storey building which may be Georgian, is The Button Queen. It is owned and operated by Martyn and Isabel Frith. Established *c.*1957, the shop specializes in antique and old buttons as well as horn and modern items and provides services to dressmakers and haberdashers.

[1] The authors are grateful to Oliver Bradbury for the use of his article on this little known novelty of Marylebone in 'Rites of Passage' in the *Marylebone Journal*, November 2006.

46. *An advertisement for Francis Edwards, bookseller at 83 Marylebone High Street c.1954, now the premises of Daunt's booksellers.*

47. *Paul Rothe's shop at 35 Marylebone Lane in 1925. On the left is Paul Rothe, and on the right his assistant, Ernie.*

Notable Buildings

The development of Marylebone, as we know it, began in 1717 with the plans for Cavendish Square *(see p. 17)*. At that time, the few notable pre-18th-century landmarks in Marylebone included Marylebone manor house, at what is now No. 60 Marylebone High Street and on which there had been a house since *c.* 1279,[1] the Lilestone Manor House, recorded in the Domesday Book, on the site of a modern office block at 191 Old Marylebone Road and the Lord Mayor's Banqueting House of 1565 (opposite Bond Street Station), demolished *c.* 1757 about the time of the development of Stratford Place.

Additionally, there were old taverns such as the Yorkshire Stingo, the Rose of Normandy *(p. 53)* and the Jew's Harp with its tea gardens *(p. 42)*.

ST MARYLEBONE CHURCH

The medieval parish church of *c*1200, dedicated to St John the Evangelist, stood near Oxford Street when the main village of Tyburn was adjacent. When the village moved northwards it left the church isolated on the main road to Oxford and prey to vandals and thieves. A new place of worship was therefore built *c.*1400 further up the Tyburn stream, dedicated to St Mary. Mary-by-the-bourne (stream) became its usual name and this also came to denote the village, instead of Tyburn. It was in this church in 1606 that Francis Bacon was married, and it was depicted by Hogarth as a scene for the marriage in his series *The Rake's Progress* of *c.*1733.

Another church was built on the same site 1741-2, but the immensely increased development and population of Marylebone in the second half of the 18th century rendered it

48. A marriage in the c.1400 Marylebone church, depicted in Hogarth's The Rake's Progress, *c. 1733.*

49. *The new church at the northern end of Marylebone High Street, built in 1741/2.*

too small. Population soared from 5,000 in the middle of the century to 63,000 in 1801 and yet another church was required.

The present parish church, designed by Thomas Hardwick (1752-1829), and consecrated on 4 February 1817, lies opposite the southern end of York Gate. Hardwick was an early tutor of J.M.W. Turner (who lived at what is now numbered 35 Harley Street) and they remained friends. Hardwick's son, Philip, was the executor of Turner's estate. The new church could seat between 3-4000 people and cost £80,000.

The gold-leafed angels supporting the cupola were sculpted by John Charles Felix Rossi,[2] who had had a studio and workshop in Marylebone. An unusual feature of the church was a number of groups of pews with their own fireplaces. The church was later enlarged. The extensive catacombs under the west side were bricked up in 1853 and in 1884 redevelopment proceeded in order, as the Rector said, 'to bring it more into harmony with the arrangements and decorations suited to the religious demands of the present day.' Later, a memorial stone was laid by Mrs Gladstone (wife of the Prime Minister), which may be seen on the outside wall of the apse.

50. *The new (and present) Marylebone parish church, designed by Thomas Hardwick and consecrated in 1817. View from York Gate.*

Alterations included the installation of mahogany choir stalls with angel ends, a marble mosaic floor and a fine marble pulpit. During the Second World War a bomb blew out the windows; these were replaced in 1949 with fragments of the original coloured glass incorporated.

Charles Wesley (1707-1788), who wrote the famous hymns *Soldiers of Christ Arise* and *Hark the Herald Angels Sing,* was buried in the churchyard, where now a memorial stone to him stands in the gardens in the High Street.

Lord Byron, born in Holles Street, was baptised here in 1788, as was Horatia, the daughter of Lord Nelson, in 1803.

Charles Dickens (1812-1870) lived nearby in Devonshire Terrace; his son was baptised in the church, described in his novel *Dombey and Son.* Robert Browning and Elizabeth Barrett were married here on 12 September 1846 to forestall Miss Barrett's father's intention to depart London with his daughter. Shortly after their marriage, they left for Italy, escaping his control. In 1949 the Browning Chapel was created at the rear of the church to commemorate their nuptials.

ALL SOULS, LANGHAM PLACE

All Souls, Langham Place was completed in 1823 at a cost of £18,323 and consecrated in November 1824. It is the last surviving church built by John Nash (1752-1835), the architect for Regent's Park and Regent Street.

The design of All Souls is highly regarded today, but the combination of Gothic spire and classical rotunda did not appeal universally at the time. Nash was criticised in March 1824 during a House of Commons debate when an MP called All Souls 'this deplorable and horrible object.' A reviewer for *The Mirror of Literature, Amusement, and Instruction* 2 August, 1828 wrote, 'To our eye, the church itself, apart from the tower, is perhaps, one of the most miserable structures in the metropolis.' A contemporary cartoon depicts Nash impaled on the spire of All Souls with the caption 'an extinguisher on a flat candlestick.' Nevertheless, eminent local residents paid large sums to have the exclusive use of particular pews in All Souls.

51. *All Souls, Langham Place.*

The church's design combined with its site (just at the curve of Langham Place) cleverly solved the visual problem of the upper part of Regent Street sweeping north-west into the straight Portland Place.

A landmine explosion on 8 December 1940 caused extensive roof damage. The congregation moved to St Peter's, Vere Street until All Souls re-opened on 29 April, 1951.

All Souls was extensively altered in the mid 1970s. The BBC used it to broadcast its daily service from 1951 to 1994, before the religious broadcasting department moved to Manchester. After the destruction by bombing of the Queen's Hall *(see p. 132)* the view of the church was spoilt by an undistinguished and out-of-scale building which replaced the Hall. Its visual profile had already been spoilt between the wars with the building of Broadcasting House to its north.

CHURCHES FOR A GROWING POPULATION

The Church Building Act of 1818 funded churches to meet the needs of London's growing population. Parliament set aside one million pounds to celebrate victory over Napoleon, and many churches, including All Souls, date from this legislation.

St. Mary's Wyndham Place was also one of these, designed by Sir Robert Smirke, the architect of the British Museum. It was constructed at a cost of £20,000 and consecrated in 1824. St Mary's setting affords an unobstructed view of the semi-circular portico and slender west tower topped with a small cupola.

St. Cyprian's Church, Clarence Gate is one of four churches in the Regent's Park area. Designed by Sir Ninian Comper and built in 1903, it is in a medieval Gothic style and was described by its architect as 'the development of a purely English parish church.' It has an impressive uncluttered interior with no pews.

All Saints is in Margaret Street. In 1841, the Cambridge Camden Society planned to build a 'Model Church' which would embody the tenets of the Society. William Butterfield, the architect of nearly one hundred churches, designed it in Gothic style; it was completed in 1859. The chancel, which occupies almost one-third of the length of the church, has been described as 'one of the most sumptuous and dramatic in London.' Responses to the church were mixed.

52. All Saints, Margaret Street, completed in 1859.

53. The interior of All Saints, designed by Butterfield.

54. *Christchurch, Cosway Street, designed by Hardwick and converted into offices in the 1980s.*

However, John Ruskin wrote:

'It is the first piece of architecture I have seen, built in modern days, which is free from all signs of timidity or incapacity ... it challenges fearless comparison with the noblest work of any time.' Pevsner commented: 'Without doubt the most remarkable and the most important church in Marylebone.'

Some of Marylebone's churches have now gone or closed such as Christchurch, Cosway Street, also designed by Thomas Hardwick, in 1825. The large attendances of over a thousand in the 19th century dwindled during the 20th. Christchurch closed in the early 1970s and was converted into offices in the 1980s.

OTHER DENOMINATIONS

The diversity of Marylebone's population is reflected in its places of worship. These include the Danish Church, Regent's Park *(see p. 46)*, the Swedish Church in Harcourt Street, the Welsh Baptist Chapel in Eastcastle Street, St James Roman Catholic Church, Spanish Place which replaced the chapel of the Spanish Embassy of 1793, the Central Synagogue, Great Portland Street and the London Central Mosque and Islamic Cultural Centre, Hanover Gate, Regent's Park.

The Central Synagogue began as a branch of the Great Synagogue of St James's Place, Aldgate. It originated in a warehouse but in the mid-19th century a handsome building was erected, its foundation stone laid by Baron Lionel De Rothschild. The present synagogue on the site is modern, having been rebuilt following bombing on 8 May 1941.

There are two other synagogues in Marylebone, the West End Great Synagogue in Great Cumberland Place (formed in 1842 and moving to its current location in 1870) by Davis and Emmanuel. It has a giant arched entrance loggia and is one of the finest of Victorian synagogues, with marble columns supporting the gallery and a central dome on four clustered piers. In Bryanston Court, is the West London Synagogue. The congregations, whether reform or otherwise, sometimes reflect the national origins of their congregations – and indeed how many generations they have been in England.

HERTFORD HOUSE

The Wallace Collection is based in Hertford House, Manchester Square, formerly known as Manchester House. During the late 18th and 19th century the Seymour-Conway family (Marquesses of Hertford) amassed the art collection which now bears the name of Richard Wallace, the natural son of the 4th Marquess. The Marquesses of Hertford descend from Edward Seymour, Duke of Somerset and Earl of

55. *Manchester House, the basis of today's Hertford House.*

56. Hertford House in Manchester Square, c.1905.

Hertford, the brother of Queen Jane Seymour and of the Lord Protector of England during the reign of Edward VI.

George Montagu, the 4th Duke of Manchester, built the house, reputedly because of the duck shooting nearby. He died in 1788 the year the Square was completed. Manchester House then became the residence of the Spanish Ambassador thus giving rise to the name of nearby Spanish Place. The house was then taken on by the Hertford family. During the time of the 2nd and 3rd Marquesses Hertford House was a centre of fashionable society. It was, however, little used by the 4th Marquess but on his death his son Richard Wallace decided to transport the collection of art and furniture from his rue Lafitte apartment to London, after the dangers and ruinous destruction to Paris in the Franco-Prussian War and the Commune of 1870.

Originally the façade of Hertford House was stone. However, Wallace decided to add a tiled smoking room (now Gallery IV), stables, and coach houses. Each wing was extended by a storey, which changed the north and south aspect, and these are now faced with red brick

rather than stone. Wallace added a portico and new conservatory and the balance of the garden became an inner courtyard and statuary garden. He also renamed the building Hertford House, to the annoyance of other members of the Hertford family who resented a natural son using the name.

On his death, Richard Wallace left his estate to his wife, who in turn, left the art and furniture to the nation in 1897, with the collection in France going to John Murray Scott, Richard Wallace's secretary and, later, her own secretary and advisor. Scott's bequest, on his death, of the French collection to Vita Sackville-West's mother, was the subject of a lawsuit. Lady Sackville prevailed: the collection was put into the hands of the dealer Jacques Seligmann and broken up. Nothing remains in Paris of the long residence of the Hertfords, save for the fountains known as Wallaces, cast and installed by Richard Wallace for the benefit of horses. There is a specimen in the front courtyard at the Wallace Collection[3]

On June 25, 1900, the Prince of Wales formally opened the Wallace Collection as a national museum.

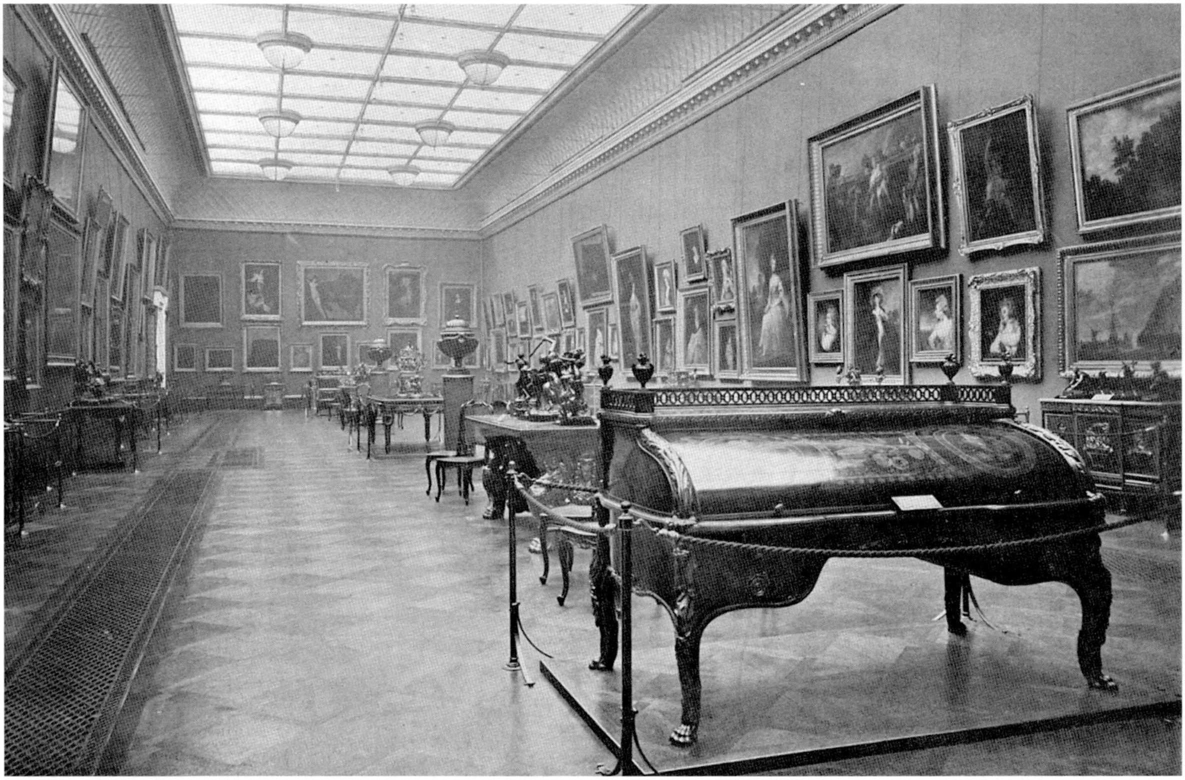

57. The Great Gallery in the Wallace Collection, c. 1896.

58. Richard Wallace sitting in the Great Gallery.

The courtyard has recently been transformed by a glass canopy and the principal rooms have been restored to a grandeur suitable for the high decorative appeal of the French furniture, particularly of the periods of Louis XIV, XV and XVI. The scale of the rooms recently redecorated in historically accurate jewel colours of lampas silk make a delicious setting, worthy of their provenance but without the 'museum' restraints.

Without the Wallace Collection, Britain's public collections would hardly do justice to the magnificence of French painting and furniture making and design of the 18th Century. The Wallace Collection "... fills that lacuna in our national possessions which was always hitherto a matter of regret", so wrote E. Beresford Chancellor in 1908, in *The Private Palaces of London Past and Present.*[4]

59. *The Langham Hotel, soon after it opened in 1865.*

THE LANGHAM HOTEL

The scale of this vast hotel is out of keeping with its surroundings but Cherry and Pevsner concede it is a fine composition. It stands on the site of Foley House *(see p 25)* demolished in 1820 to make way for the construction of the mansion of Sir James Langham. Foley Street was re-named Langham Place.

The influx of visitors to London for the Great Exhibition in 1851 and the Brompton Exhibition of 1862 highlighted the shortage of hotel accommodation in London. The capital of a sprawling Empire could generally only muster inns, taverns and clubs, but these were unsuitable for women.

Following the formation of the Langham Hotel Company with capital of £150,000 from its shareholders who had purchased shares for £10, work began in July 1863. The directors held an architectural competition in 1862 won by John Giles of Craven Street in October 1862. The drawing for the main elevation was exhibited at the Royal Academy and the foundation stone was laid by the Earl of Shrewsbury and Talbot, the chairman of the Langham Hotel Company. James Murray of Portman Street, responsible for the Westminster Palace Hotel in Buckingham Gate, was hired to design the interiors and Owen Jones, whose design books included research into all of the great decorative designs of world art and who had been Superintendent of the 1851 Great Exhibition, was also hired to assist with the interiors. Jones was famous for his vivid colour schemes and open flat-patterned decorative flower designs.[5] Ultimately,the construction cost double the capital originally raised, that is £300,000.

The Langham, opened on 10 June, 1865, was intended to be the first continental style luxury hotel in London. It was to have the latest and best engineering including hydraulic lifts, superior fire proofing and protection, modern plumbing and air conditioning. There were 14 public lavatories and nearly 300 water closets. By way of comparison, in 1856, the Exeter Hotel in the Strand offered one water closet per floor. In the externally grand St. Pancras Hotel (part opened 1873), there were no ensuite bathrooms or lavatories.

The *Building News* expounded on the services provided for the sophisticated clientele: post and telegraph office, libraries, newsagent, reading rooms, billiard rooms, parcels rooms. Also visitors could bring domestic pets but 'only small dogs' could share the rooms with their owners.

The Langham afforded a 'home away from home' and many rich families, without a house in town, stayed there for the season instead of renting a house. The exiled Emperor of France, Louis Napoleon III, lived there for the last years of his life.

By the 1890s, while the Langham made much of its solid, well-established and reassuring comfort and personal service, more upbeat competitors were appearing on the scene. Its success brought competition: the Savoy opened in 1889, Claridges was rebuilt between 1895-9, and the Ritz opened in 1906. The Langham's answer was to emphasise its traditional comforts and service, while nevertheless bringing in new technology. It introduced electric lighting throughout in 1888 and was the first hotel to do this.

Arthur Conan Doyle featured the Langham in several short stories starting with *A Scandal in Bohemia* (1891). He wanted his characters to stay in a stylish hotel.

The hotel's artistic clientele was not always of unlimited means: the Czech composer Antonin Dvorak caused a stir when he asked if he could share a double room with his grown-up daughter. The management declined this arrangement.

Oscar Wilde, in the late 1880s and early 1890s, after the success of his plays *An Ideal Husband, Lady Windermere's Fan* and *The Importance of Being Earnest*, frequented the Langham though his own conduct and that of the literati with whom he socialised may have conflicted with the bourgeois formality of other guests.

The conductor, Arturo Toscanini, stayed there, but distinguished himself on one occasion when, impatient with a journalist, he is alleged to have beaten him with a stick in the foyer.

The actor and playwright Noel Coward, film actress Anna Neagle, the variety artist and singer Gracie Fields and in 1930 the Australian cricket team led by Don Bradman, then at the height of his formidable powers, were all guests and even habitués. Discretion was required for the visits arranged for Mrs Wallis Warfield Simpson. At the time of the abdication of Edward VIII, she took a house nearby in Regent's Park.

The Second World War saw the end of its fashionable heyday. On the night of 16 September 1940, a bomb destroyed much of the west wing of the building and further serious damage was done in subsequent air-raids when the water tank on top of the building was fractured. The writer, J.B. Priestley, was staying at the Langham that night, went across the road to the BBC to make a broadcast and on his return found that his room was in the wing destroyed in the meantime. The Langham closed as a hotel.

After the war, parts of the Langham became offices and studios, and overnight accommodation for the BBC's broadcasters and guests. The BBC considered at various times buying the building – it was by no means ideal for broadcasting but many popular radio programmes went out from there.

In 1986, the Ladbroke Group plc bought the Langham and in 1987 work began to restore it. The hotel, refurbished at a cost of £80 million, re-opened as the Langham Hilton in 1991.

60. Quintin Hogg, founder of the Regent Street Polytechnic.

61. The Polytechnic in its early years.

THE LANDMARK HOTEL

Formerly the Great Central Hotel, an adjunct to Marylebone Station at its rear, was designed by Robert Edis *(see p. 82)*.

STRATFORD HOUSE

Stratford House, built *c.* 1774, (the home of the Oriental Club since 1 January 1962), sits at the centre of Stratford Place and is sometimes attributed to Robert Adam, but it was designed by Richard Edwin.[6] Edward Stratford (later the 2nd Earl of Aldborough) bought the site of Stratford Place from the City of London which had once used the Tyburn stream there to form a conduit to serve the City *(see p9)*.

The house remained as it was built until 1894 when the owner, Murray Guthrie, installed new plumbing and strengthened the under-pinning to take the weight of a second storey which he had built to both the east and west wings. This was the first alteration to the external appearance. The next owner, Sir Edward (later Baron) Colebrook in 1903 undertook a reconstruction to a 'complete Adam design' of the library. In 1908, Lord Derby bought the lease and altered the house further, removing the central bifurcated staircase and replacing it with a space-saving single staircase. In 1959-1960, the house was purchased by the Oriental Club then in Hanover Square. The Club was founded in 1824 by Sir John Malcolm with the Duke of Wellington as Honorary President and with members drawn from the East India Company and officials in public service in India. Members today are active in industry, commerce the civil service and professions.

REGENT STREET POLYTECHNIC AND TWO FAMOUS COLLEGES

In 1838 the Polytechnic Institution was founded by George Cayley at 309 Regent Street. It closed its doors in 1881, when the premises were purchased by the merchant and philanthropist, Quintin Hogg (1845-1903) who had founded a Young Men's Christian Institute *c.* 1870. Hogg, who lived at 5 Cavendish Square, retained the word Polytechnic and the Institute became known as the Regent Street Polytechnic.

When Hogg died suddenly in 1903, he was succeeded as president by Kynaston Studd who carried on the vision of the founder which gave equal prominence to learning and to sport. The Polytechnic was rebuilt 1910-12 and an extension was opened in Little Titchfield Street in 1929. It is now part of the University of Westminster.

A statue of Quintin Hogg is in Portland Place. Marylebone is home also to two famous colleges, Queen's College and the Royal Academy of Music.

Queen's College in Harley Street was founded in 1848 and was the first to provide further education for women, in particular for the benefit of potential governesses. Three men were prominent in its foundation – Frederick Denison Maurice and Charles Kingsley, who both helped to found the Working Men's College in Holborn, and also the Rev. David Laing, an energetic Kentish Town clergyman who was enormously helpful to the young Frances Buss, herself a pupil at Queen's, when she began her Camden School for Girls, a landmark venture in women's education.

Since the last war Queen's has been an independent day school for girls, with about 380 students.

The Royal Academy of Music in Marylebone Road has its origins in a meeting of noblemen at the Thatched House Tavern in St James's in July 1822. Activities began in a house in Tenterden Street, Hanover Square, but unpromisingly there were only 21 pupils and they were all under the age of 12. Fanny, sister of Charles Dickens, was a pupil in this very under-resourced school. Things did not improve until 1868 when Gladstone gave it a grant and it expanded, increased its prestige and reputation and in 1912 opened its large building in the Marylebone Road, designed by Sir Ernest George and Albert Yates. The Academy is now a constituent part of the University of London.

ST MARYLEBONE GRAMMAR SCHOOL

In 1792 a group of philanthropically motivated men, among whom was Thomas Collingwood, founded a school at 1 Mary Street (now Stanhope Street, Fitzrovia) for the deserving poor. The school, supported by subscription, was called the Philological Society and had an initial intake of 40 boys. A new prospectus was drawn up in 1800 which stressed the aims of instilling piety and the habits of industry. The school moved to what is now 248 Marylebone Road (then 36 New Road) in 1827[7].

The headmaster for forty-five years, Edwin Abbott, emphasised moral values and duty.

62. St Marylebone Grammar School c. 1780

Corporal punishment was to be administered by him in his discretion. In 1882, Sidney Webb became chairman of the London County Council Technical Education Board which commissioned a survey of London education. The TEB, while recognizing the work of the Philological Society, recommended wider advertisement of the school and its services in order to increase the number of students paying the fees, but by the end of the century the TEB was recommending a state controlled secondary education system in the hands of local authorities.

The School's name was changed to St Marylebone Grammar School for Boys in 1901; its headmaster, William Moore, who had been there since 1848, resigned citing his age and lack of enthusiasm for implementing momentous change; the numbers of pupils continued to decline and on 1 January 1909 the LCC took over administration. In 1920, G.S. Penny was appointed headmaster and he secured many innovations and impressive improvements to the school enabling its academic achievement to grow. However, his headship came to an abrupt end when, under pressure of exhaustion and anxiety, he threw himself and his three-year-old daughter over a balcony at their flat in Elgin Avenue. The daughter did not survive. Mr. Penny was sentenced to be detained in Broadmoor.

Lord Rothermere, a former pupil, made a gift of £10,000, which a new headmaster put to good use. Rothermere continued to make substantial donations and by 1928, the school was making academic progress. After the Second World War, during which pupils were moved to Cornwall, a plan to close the school and open a new one for 1,250 students in the St. John's Wood area became one of national interest: as the school had provided independent education for pupils for so many years, there was doubt as to the benefits of change. In 1953, the school was saved and designated as Voluntary Controlled, whereupon its long serving headmaster, Philip Wayne retired; its new headmaster, Harry Llewellen-Smith, served until 1970 and the school was further expanded.

63. *Broadcasting House between the wars.*

In 1970, the Inner London Education Authority proposed a merger with a local secondary modern school. This politically sensitive move was resisted, but by 1981 the Grammar School was closed. The Asda Group acquired the building on Marylebone Road, and restored it. It is now Grade II listed.

Famous alumni were Jerome K Jerome (author of *Three Men in a Boat*), the author and historian Eric Hobsbawm, the novelists Len Deighton and Patrick O Brian, footballer John Barnes and circus entrepreneur Bertram Mills.

BROADCASTING HOUSE
The building itself is out of scale. Cherry and Pevsner[8] complain of its 'lumpish appearance' and that it deprives All Souls of 'its subtle siting value'. It was designed by Lt. Colonel G. Val Myer with sculptures of Prospero and Ariel on the exterior by Eric Gill. It is famously related that when Gill worked on a scaffold to sculpt the

64. Architect's drawing for Abbey House at the top end of Baker Street.

65. While the rest of the building was being redeveloped in 2007, the famous tower was supported.

figures he wore a smock but no underclothes and provided unconventional entertainment for passers-by. Basically the structure is a building within a building, initially with a central tower of 22 studios surrounded by offices which helped to insulate sound.

The BBC had begun its first regular transmissions on 14 November 1922; by 1927, it had grown out of its premises at Savoy Hill and was searching for new headquarters. Fortuitously, Lord Waring wished to sell his property at the southern end of Portland Place, providing an ideal location. The BBC first transmitted from Broadcasting House on 15 May 1932. On Christmas Day that year, King George V gave the first broadcast to the Empire.

In October 1940, a bomb fell on Broadcasting House, killing seven staff. The building had a concrete structure known as *The Stronghold* to allow broadcasting to continue in such eventualities, and it did. Room 101 (now demolished) was apparently the inspiration for the scenes of torture in Orwell's dystopian novel of the future, *1984*. Orwell, who worked at the BBC during the 1940s, commented that it was: 'A cross between a girls' school and a lunatic asylum.'

THE ABBEY BUILDING AND 221b BAKER STREET

The Abbey Road Building Society was established in 1849 as the National Freehold Land and Building Society and its new headquarters, Abbey House, opened in Baker Street in March 1932. It shares the address with Arthur Conan Doyle's famous character. Abbey commissioned from the sculptor, John

Doubleday, a bronze statue of Sherlock Holmes to stand at the entrance to Baker Street underground station. The statue was unveiled in September 1999 to commemorate Abbey's 150th anniversary.

Abbey moved its head office in 2002 and its landmark building is being redeveloped, but the distinctive façade and tower are being retained in a complex operation.

ROYAL INSTITUTE OF BRITISH ARCHITECTS

The Royal Institute of British Architects was formed in 1834, receiving a Royal Charter in 1837. Its headquarters at 66 Portland Place, on the corner of Weymouth Street, is a Grade II-listed building, designed by Grey Wornum (1888-1957), the winner of the competition for the design. The building, on the Howard de Walden Estate, was opened by King George V on 8 November 1934, appropriately in the centenary year of the Institute. (RIBA were granted a 999-year lease, which was a policy of the Estate at the time.)[9]

The building is to scale with its John Nash neighbours unlike the 20th-century flats nearby. No. 12 Weymouth Street is an example of the Georgian buildings – 62-68 Portland Place – which were demolished to make way for the RIBA building. It houses an extensive architectural library.

Although the building has had its severe critics, the opinion of Maxwell Fry (1899-1987), a leading British architect and champion of modernism, was that its great achievement was

"the imaginative handling of staircase levels which command views both upward and downward of great richness and complexity".

The building uses rich and exotic materials. Wornum had led the Architectural Association excursion to Stockholm in 1930 and may have been influenced by Ragnar Ostberg the architect of the Stockholm Town Hall, to wit, a re-working of neo-classicism, economical fenestration, sumptuous use of rich materials (so characteristic of Swedish design) especially marble and exotic timbers. The styles of the 1930s

66. *The RIBA building in Portland Place.*

fell out of favour and it is only since the late '70s, with the revival of interest in such buildings and their architectural sources, that this building's strengths have been appreciated.[10]

[1] Ann Saunders, *Regent's Park from 1086 to the present* (rev. edn), 17

[2] See p. 42

[3] The best book on the history of the Wallace Collection is Donald Mallett, *The Greatest Collector, Lord Hertford and the Founding of the Wallace Collection* (1980).

[4] The authors are grateful to Oliver Bradbury for the use of his article in the *Marylebone Journal* (Winter 2005) for bringing this quotation and other useful information to their attention.

[5] Many of his designs were revived by Zoffany in the early 1980s.

[6] Gordon Mackenzie, *Marylebone, Great City North of Oxford Street* (1972), 90.

[7] E.G.B. Neal, *St Marylebone Grammar School, a brief History until 1954.*

[8] Bridget Cherry and Nikolaus Pevsner, *Buildings of England, London, No. 3* (1991), 650.

[9] Info. Richard Bowden, Archivist, Howard de Walden Estate.

[10] Oliver Bradbury in *Marylebone Journal*, March 2007.

Two Principal Roads

THE NEW ROAD

In 1756 construction began on a major road from Paddington to The Angel, Islington called, for want of a better name, the New Road. A hundred years later it was nominally sectioned into three, Marylebone Road, Euston Road and Pentonville Road. At the time it was London's first bypass, providing a wide road that allowed the movement of cattle and other animals from the country down to Smithfield without going into the crowded and narrow streets of the West End and the City. It also enabled, the sponsors of the Road asserted, the free movement of troops in emergencies. The Duke of Bedford, whose town house was in Bloomsbury, some distance from the road, protested against what he thought would be disturbance from the traffic, but most of the land holders along the route were happy since it would lead inevitably to development along it. The road's presence at Paddington was no doubt a factor in determining the extent of the Grand Union Canal in 1801, for it meant that goods unloaded at the canal Basin there could be transported on to a decent road for distribution.

The Act of Parliament allowing this development stipulated that the roadway was to be 40ft wide and that houses should be set back 50 foot from the highway, a requirement that has enabled successive authorities to widen the road as need demanded it.

Wellington's victory at Waterloo in 1815 required permanent commemoration. Several schemes were put forward for monuments in London: indeed it was even proposed to name what became Regent's Park after him, but the Prince Regent had no intention of agreeing to that.[1] Another scheme, proposed by John Martin in 1820, was to span the New Road at its junction with Portland Place with a triumphal arch. The public would have access to a viewing platform surmounted by a statue of the 'Iron Duke'.

The introduction of horse buses in England is generally regarded as having happened on 4 July 1829 when George Shillibeer (1797-1866) ran a service from Paddington Green, via the Yorkshire Stingo near Lisson Grove in Marylebone, along the New Road and eventually down to the Bank.

Shillibeer was a Londoner, born in Tottenham

67. George Shillibeer's Omnibus.

68. *The upper part of Baker Street c.1905, with what is now Melcombe Street on the left.*

Court Road, and a maverick. He learned his trade building coaches while living in Paris and received a commission to build a vehicle which, as in France, was called an 'omnibus'. His design, however, was not new. It resembled a stretched stage coach; had a flat roof, a door at the rear, and could take 18 passengers. It was drawn by three horses abreast. Inside were banquette seats running the length of the vehicle so that passengers faced each other. Unlike stage coaches, his omnibuses ran to a fixed timetable which included taking up and setting down frequently en route at what were known, nevertheless, as 'stages'. An onboard conductor collected fares and assisted passengers on and off. The whole journey – it cost one shilling – took between 40 minutes and an hour.

Shillibeer's operation was a success until competition cut his profits and by 1831 he became bankrupt. In the same year a consortium of horse bus owners was created to limit competition and Shillibeer was elected chairman. He fell into bad financial straits again, fled the country and on his return he found himself in prison for smuggling brandy.

On release Shillibeer become an undertaker, a financially less risky occupation and invented a funeral coach. He is remembered by Shillibeer Place close to the site of the *Yorkshire Stingo* .

The New Road was used by the government as a barrier in the railway age, when it stipulated that no railway line should cross it. This resulted in the string of main line stations along its route.

BAKER STREET

Baker Street was originally divided into Baker Street and Upper Baker Street, but in March 1930 the two were amalgamated and comprehensively renumbered.

The road was laid out from 1755 by William Baker, a property developer who leased the land from the Portman Estate. It has since been substantially redeveloped and its frontages are mostly shops and offices, with most of the earlier four and five-storey Georgian terraced housing displaced. No.120 was the home 1802-6 of William Pitt the Younger (1759-1806). Other notable residents include the writer Bulwer Lytton (1803-73) who was born at No. 68, the essayist, traveller and scholar Sir Richard Burton

69. *Chiltern Court above Baker Street station, originally intended as an hotel.*

(1821-1890), and the actress Sarah Siddons (1755-1831) who lived in a house (now demolished) in what was Upper Baker Street.

Burton was a multi-lingual product of an Empire which provided opportunities for many eccentrics, but inspired people like him to be themselves. Burton had an Indian mistress and he married an intrepid woman who learned to fence in order, as she put it, 'to defend Richard if he is attacked'. He enjoyed baiting missionaries and those he considered socialists or democrats. One of his more admirable traits was to buy caged birds in order to set them free. The author of fifty books of unreliable spelling, he had a publishing company with the impressive name 'The Kama Shastra Society of London and Benares' based in Stoke Newington. He possessed an impressive collection of literature of an explicitly sexual nature.

Burton was buried at Mortlake in a mausoleum designed as a Bedouin tent.

The vicinity of Baker Street contains blocks of mansion flats. The mansion flat was an invention of the late Victorian period, intended to deal with the need for dense residential development, while allaying the fears of the middle classes of living in multiple occupancy buildings where they had to share hallways and stairways. More to the point for some, they could be managed without the necessity of live-in servants who were increasingly difficult to find or afford.

An imposing example is Chiltern Court in Baker Street, designed by C.W. Clark 1913-1915, and completed as flats in 1929. It lies over Baker Street Station and integrated as part of it. Originally intended as a hotel, work was disrupted by the First World War.

[1] Ann Saunders, *Regent's Park from 1086 to the Prresent* (rev. edn. 1981), 111

Lisson Green

The Domesday Book of 1086 mentions Lisson Green as the manor of Lilestone. The manor developed as a hamlet with its manor house lying to the east side of Edgware Road, the boundary with Paddington, with another small settlement to the west. Old Marylebone Road, then called Watery Lane, formed the south-west extent of the manor and the Tyburn stream provided the boundary on the east. What became St John's Wood was to the north.

The rapid development of London from 1720 turned Lisson Green from rural obscurity to a service and labour provider, enhanced by the construction of the New Road (Marylebone Road) in 1756.

No.191 Old Marylebone Road, which cuts off at an angle almost as a continuation of Lisson Grove and then becomes Sussex Gardens, is the site of the original Lilestone manor house (sometimes known as Lisson Green manor house. Its earliest construction is not known, but it was rebuilt in 1791 by the MP, John Harcourt. In

1813, the house was sold to Queen Charlotte's Hospital founded about sixty years earlier as the 'General Lying in Hospital'. A further rebuilding took place in 1856.

After the hospital relocated, the site was occupied by St Dunstan's, the charity which was originally housed after the First World War in St Dunstan's Villa in Regent's Park *(see p. 47)*. The charity is devoted to helping people with visual impairment. It moved from 191 Old Marylebone Road in 1984 after which the present (wretched) building on the site was erected.

AN ARTISTS' COMMUNITY

Lisson Grove, for its cleaner air, attracted some well-to-do residents and a number of artists. Richard Cosway may have had a studio in Stafford Street (now Cosway Street).[1] Cosway (1742-1821) arrived in London in or about December 1754 and lodged originally with the drawing master William Shipley, the founder of the Society for the Encouragement of the Arts, Manufactures and Commerce, for the next five years.

Samuel Palmer (1805-1881), pre-eminently the

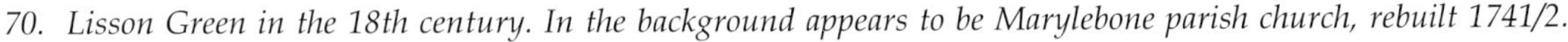

70. Lisson Green in the 18th century. In the background appears to be Marylebone parish church, rebuilt 1741/2.

71. The Yorkshire Stingo,[2] a prominent and popular building in Lisson Green, is mentioned in rate books in 1684, and was probably visited twice by Pepys in 1666 accompanied by a female. The site of the inn was partly taken by the Church Army building on the south side of the Marylebone Road. Stingo is a term for a strong ale. The site was sold in the 1850s to Marylebone Vestry.

creator of the so-called 'visionary landscape', sent in pictures to the Royal Academy when residing at 4 Grove Street, Lisson Grove from 1832-42. The street no longer exists.

He and John Linnell (1792-1882) were influenced by and friendly with William Blake. The group sometimes called themselves the 'Old Water-Colour Society' and attracted literary figures of the early romantic movement including Wordsworth, Keats and Charles Lamb to dinner parties and other social events.

Benjamin Haydon (1786-1846) was another member of Lisson Grove's artistic community. He rented a house at what was then 22 Lisson Grove North[3] from John Charles Felix Rossi *(see p 42)* to produce works of vast dimensions featuring heroic and monumental subjects .

In 1827, ruminating over the lack of recognition and material success, he intoned: "My 'Judgement of Solomon' is rolled up in a warehouse in the borough! My 'Entry to Jerusalem' is doubled up in a back room in Holborn! My 'Lazarus' is in an upholsterer's shop in Mount Street and my 'Crucifixion' is in a hay-loft in Lisson Grove!" His misery culminated in suicide. A blue plaque at No. 116 Lisson Grove commemorates his life and work.

THE PORTMAN MARKET

Portman Market was sited on a square, three-acre site on the north side of Church Street between Penfold and Salisbury Streets. Originally a hay market opened in 1830, it later became a vegetable and general market and included buildings and abattoirs. The Portmans were the estate owners. The market was intended as a rival for this part of London to Covent Garden. It was taken over and rebuilt by H.T. Gunton in 1900, but it did not prosper and was sold in 1906. It became a maintenance depot but was bombed during the Second World War. Later the site was redeveloped as part of the Church Street Estate of municipal housing.[4]

TWO DEPARTMENT STORES

Lisson Green developed its own shopping precinct. Between 1885 and 1889 Richard Jordan was a pawnbroker at 19-21 Church Street. By 1925 his grandson William Jordan had taken over 23 Church Street and the Mitre pub site as a clothier and house furnisher and by 1928, numbers 13-17 were included; over 80 people were employed during the 1940s. In 1976 the store closed and was redeveloped as Alfie's Antique Market, which is under the same management and ownership as Gray's Antique Market in Davies Street.

Spence Turner & Boldero began as a linen draper's, taking over first numbers 60-74 Lisson Grove and later 75-93 to become a department store and wholesale warehouse. At one point it employed 300 assistants and 200 needlewomen and had a staff dining room and reading room. The building was demolished in 1970 and is replaced by social housing and a social security office.

THE HOUSES

Survivors of Lisson Green's more prosperous past may be seen in attractive early 19th-century houses at Nos 95-135 Lisson Grove and in Broadley Street and 5-18 Cosway Street and the east end of Church Street.

By the 1830s, however, parts of the district were built up with cheap and shoddily

72. Church Street Market, 2007.

constructed dwellings for rent. The journalist and novelist George Sala (1828-1896) described Lisson Green in 1868:

> Although situated in one of the most beautiful outskirts of London, and environed by districts of well-built homes inhabited by the most respectable middle-class families, the 'Grove' itself bore a most unenviable reputation … it was one of the chosen resorts of the 'dangerous classes' … Before the establishment of the new police, if some distinguished member of the light-fingered class, or heavy-crowbarred fraternity was 'wanted'; if Web-Footed Joe was anxiously looked after in connection with a number of gold watches, then it was to the neighbourhood of Lisson Green that the (police) were wont to pay their attention.

Sala also provides a vivid description of the street:

> …the Grove appeared to me in the guise of a most objectionable thicket, in which rags, old boots and shoes, defunct cats, and tin saucepans fallen into desuetude were to be found … Hulking men in corduroy with short pipes in their mouths and their hands in their pockets; slatternly women and neglected children sprawling in the gutter, half-starved sparrows, consumptive chickens and ravenous dogs were the chief contribution to animated nature in the Grove. The principal public buildings were pawnbokers … low public houses and beershops, and cheap undertakers. There hung about the place a faint odour of fried fish and adulterated Geneva.[5] The only vehicles seen within the precinct were coster-mongers' barrows, the police-stretcher, and the workhouse-sedan. They used to fight a great deal in Lisson Grove in those days; black eyes were very much 'worn' – especially on Monday mornings.

POVERTY AND HOUSING REFORM

Blame for the decline of the area was placed on itinerant labourers (originally Irish) who came to work on the railroads and canals, especially the Regent's Canal which fully opened in 1820. They arrived in England in large numbers, in particular during 1845-1849, the years of the famine in Ireland caused by the potato blight .

They took employment with wages and conditions poorer than local labourers were prepared to accept. At the time much of Ireland was owned by absentee landlords (including the Marquesses of Hertford who owned 60,000 acres) intent on maximising rental income – the plight of their tenants little concerned them.

The slum clearance that resulted from the construction of Shaftesbury Avenue, Charing Cross Road and New Oxford Street in the 1870s meant that their inhabitants found accommodation elsewhere, particularly in the Lisson Grove area where housing was cheap but poor.

Charles Booth the author of *Life and Labour of the People of London* published in 1903 identified some of the worst pockets of deprivation around Bell Street and what is now Ranston Street (formerly Charles Street). The story of Eliza Armstrong who lived in one room at 32 Charles Street with her parents, brothers and sister is described on p. 110.

In 1895, Octavia Hill managed to get the slums in this street cleared and replaced with the present Almond & St. Botolph's Cottages.

THE COMING OF THE GREAT CENTRAL RAILWAY

The Manchester, Sheffield & Lincoln Railway Company built an eastern extension for goods and passengers into London. The construction, of the terminus and its connected hotel, now the Landmark on Marylebone Road are described on p. 82.

Fifty-one acres were required involving the purchase of small freeholds of residential property including slum dwellings. There was some requirement for the Company to rehouse the displaced, which resulted in the erection of six tenement blocks, named Wharncliffe Gardens, to house 2,690, on St John's Wood Road.

CROCKER'S FOLLY

Now little noticed in the Marylebone Road because of its site just before the flyover, is a very original set of flats in the Arts and Crafts style designed by Gordon & Gunton, stone faced with an arcaded top floor and with bas relief stylised carving around the bay windows.

The Crown Hotel in Aberdeen Place, off the Edgware Road, was built in 1898-9 by a noted architect, C.H. Worley *(see p. 28)* for Frank Crocker, a local publican. He hoped to benefit from the Great Central Railway, anticipating the terminus being close by. Based on this, his building project was grand. However, plans changed and the terminus opened – but a mile away! Crocker was bankrupted.

The building is a magnificent example of Victorian pub architecture with splendid plasterwork, woodwork and marble ornamentation. 'Crocker's Folly' as it was dubbed, soldiered on for many years, gradually decaying, until the 1980s when it underwent refurbishment and was officially renamed 'Crocker's Folly'. Currently (as of September 2007) boarded up, it is to be hoped that the building will find another use.

[1] Richard Cosway lived in Berkeley Street (1768), Pall Mall from 1784 in Schomberg House, and on the corner of Oxford Street and Stratford Place from 1791 until 1821.

[2] The fullest account of the Yorkshire Stingo is in E. Bright Ashford, *Lisson Green* (1960) published by the St Marylebone Society.

[3] Erica McDonald and David J. Smith, *Pineapples & Pantomimes, a history of Church Street and Lisson Green* (1992). Published by City of Westminster Libraries.

[4] *Ibid*, 18

[5] Gin.

Canal and Railways

By 1750, although many of the country's major roads had been converted into turnpikes, the carriage of goods overland was still slow, expensive and unreliable. A faster form of transport was needed especially for the essential materials which England's great cities and their expanding populations needed. Early proposals for canals included several to join the West Midlands and Birmingham with London and, additionally, to link such a canal to the Thames. London was the busiest port in the world. In 1790, Birmingham was joined indirectly to the London area via the Oxford Canal and the Thames. In 1793, the construction of a canal was authorised to link the Oxford Canal at Braunston in Northamptonshire via a more direct route through the Chilterns to the Thames at Brentford. Additions to the scheme for a new 'Grand Union Canal' resulted in a branch terminating at Paddington and a continuation of the new canal skirting round north London to the River Lea and from there to the Thames to the east of London. This extension would give access to the London docks.

The branch to Paddington opened in 1801 and was immediately successful. A London entrepreneur, Thomas Homer, first seriously examined the feasibility of a canal link from Paddington to the Thames at Limehouse. In 1802, he engaged the well-known canal builder, John Rennie, to survey a possible route. Rennie was optimistic about the potential traffic, but his route would have threaded its way through parts of central London and would have been too expensive. The project lay dormant for a few years, but the continuing success of the Paddington branch led Homer to pursue the matter. In 1810, he proposed a route avoiding central London passing, instead, through a largely undeveloped area north of the New Road (now the Marylebone Road) from Paddington, via Marylebone to Islington. The Duke of Portland's lease on much of the land in this area

was about to expire and the Crown Commissioners wished to develop the area then known as Marylebone Park. In 1811 Homer began discussions with John Nash who, as noted on p.43, was drawing up plans, with the encouragement and patronage of the Prince Regent, to develop parts of Marylebone Park for residential use. Homer and Nash estimated the annual tonnage and receipts of the proposed canal. Based on this, Nash invested his own money in the project which by now was unofficially called the 'Regent's Canal'. Homer subsequently turned out to be a fraudster and when his activities were discovered he was tried, convicted and sentenced to seven years' transportation to Australia.

The canal would leave the Grand Union at Paddington Basin and cross land owned by the Bishop of London, partly in a tunnel. In a north-easterly direction, it would curve under Edgware Road and thread through parts of the estates belonging to the Eyre and Portman families and to Harrow School. It would then skirt the north side of Marylebone Park before turning further north and pass through Camden Town and then turn south-east towards Islington, Haggerston, Mile End and Limehouse at which point it would join the Thames. In the initial plans the canal passed through the centre of Marylebone Park. Nash thought the water and the passage of boats would be an attractive element for the Park, but the Commissioners of Woods and Forests did not agree and a revised plan had it along the northern perimeter of the Park.

There was opposition to the new canal. Some argued that this linear 'pond' of stagnant water would have a harmful effect on the health of those living nearby. Others anticipated possible disruption to the natural springs coming to the surface in the area north of the New Road where the level (but gently rising) ground on which Marylebone is built meets the lower slopes of the Northern Ridge of London. The men employed as wharfingers at the Paddington Basin said the new canal would reduce the cargo being loaded and unloaded at that point. Others pointed out the conflict of interest of Nash being engaged in

73. *Macclesfield Bridge on the Regent's Canal, c.1830, by Thomas H. Shepherd.*

an official capacity, but also having a private investment in the new canal.

Many landowners along the route of the canal received compensation for the surrender of their land. Among these was Thomas Lord who received £4,000 for relinquishing his second cricket ground *(see p. 39).*

By 1816 the company promoting the canal was in financial trouble, made worse by the economic crisis following the end of the Napoleonic wars. The recession not only restricted the amount of money available for investment but also led to large-scale unemployment and hardship in London. Nash was a proponent of an idea to gain official subsidies for the canal company while at the same time obtaining a reliable supply of unskilled labour. He proposed that a weekly levy should be imposed on whatever wage the paupers were paid for their labour. The canal company would then use the levy to buy the men pick-axes when the job was finished. These men, with their labouring experience, and now owners of the tools of their trade, would then find work and

cease to be a public burden. For their part, the government and the poor law authorities, anticipating relief from the burden of the unemployed, would express their thanks in generous financing for the company

Nash's idea was never put to the test. The economy recovered and the canal was built and fully opened in 1820. It was never the financial success its investors had hoped. It was a late arrival on the canal scene and soon railways proved serious competitors. In 1845 the directors of the Regent's Canal considered a scheme for converting it into a railway which would connect the lines of the Great Western, the London & Birmingham and the Eastern Counties Railways. First provisionally titled the London Junction Railway Company and then the Regent's Canal Railway Company, the project capsized in 1846 when the speculative railway boom collapsed. The Regent's Canal Company then proposed to build a railway supplementing the canal and located alongside it. This was to run from Paddington station connecting with all other lines en route to Limehouse, but the residents of

74. *The Gunpowder Explosion disaster on the Regent's Canal in 1874. As depicted in the* Illustrated London News.

Regent's Park had no wish for their shining stucco to be besmirched by smoke and smuts from coal powered locomotives. When the Government opposed a railway in the vicinity of the Park, the scheme was dropped.

EXPLOSION AT MACCLESFIELD BRIDGE
Macclesfield Bridge, named after the Earl of Macclesfield (a director of the canal company), spans the canal at its north-west corner. In the early hours of 2 October 1874 a steam tug was hauling five barges from the City Basin in a westerly direction towards Paddington. They were loaded with grain, sugar, petroleum and general cargo but the third barge, *Tilbury*, contained five pounds of gunpowder. Just before 5am as the flotilla passed under the Macclesfield Bridge an explosion threw out mud, brick, stone and iron-work, pieces of timber from the barges and branches from trees. Flames from a gas main fractured by the blast illuminated the scene and widespread structural damage was caused to buildings as far as a mile away. Part of the keel of the *Tilbury* fell onto the roof of a house three hundred metres away landing with such force that it fell through to the basement. The commanding officer at the Albany Street Barracks, convinced that the explosion was the work of Irish nationalists, ordered his men – armed– down to the canal. Of the three-man crew of the *Tilbury*, no trace was found. The men on the other barges survived.

Crowds rushed to the scene in the midst of attempts to find survivors or recover bodies and horse buses and trains serving the area could hardly cope with the people who wished to view the disaster.

The explosion had been caused by vapour from the petroleum being ignited by the fire in the stove on board the *Tilbury*. The disaster highlighted the dangers of moving volatile substances through populated areas of the Metropolis. Few could believe that the men working the barges habitually warmed themselves with the heat from a stove inches away from such flammable substances. Some people still refer to the rebuilt Macclesfield Bridge as 'Blow Up Bridge'.

The Regent's Canal may not have rewarded the financial hopes of its early investors but it nevertheless carried fuels, raw materials and many other items without further major incident. It has enjoyed a renaissance over the last fifty years, being used by pleasure craft and, now of course – as the prescient Nash thought it would — it provides a pleasant scenic feature along this built up area of London. Living nearby and in particular overlooking the reflective calm of the Regent's Canal is a benefit. The Canal and the paths along it suit the needs of Londoners for a traffic-free place to walk. Although there are some of the usual city problems, even local authorities have come to appreciate the benefits.

THE FIRST UNDERGROUND RAILWAY
As well as being on the route of the first omnibus service in London (*see p 70*) Marylebone was one of the areas served by the Metropolitan Railway, the first underground railway in the world. It opened to the public on 10 January 1863, from Paddington to Farringdon, with stops at Edgware Road, Baker Street and Great Portland Street. Its intention, apart from relieving congestion on the roads, was to link some principal overland railways lining Marylebone-Euston-Pentonville Roads. At that time Marylebone Station had not yet been built and no doubt, if it had been, an attempt would have been made to connect to that as well, in the same way as Euston Square station serves Euston station – by a short walk.

There had been a number of suggestions for an intra-London railway, few of them practicable. The most important promoter of schemes was the City of London's own Solicitor, Charles Pearson (1793-1862) who, with much tenacity pushed through the final scheme but, sadly, died a year before it opened.

The idea of such a railway was of particular interest to the Great Western with its terminus at Paddington, opened in 1838, a location inconvenient for passengers travelling to and from the City. In 1854, a plan was published for a line running under Marylebone Road and linking Paddington, Euston and King's Cross and by 1858 this proposal had undergone changes so that there would be more stations and as Pearson had proposed, would turn south after King's Cross to terminate at Farringdon, on the fringe of the City.

The involvement of the Great Western meant that mixed gauge track had to be laid, as this company used a unique broad gauge of a fraction over 7 feet associated with Isambard Kingdom Brunel whereas other possible partners adhered to the standard gauge. Great concerns were expressed, even at this early stage, about the fire hazards arising from the use of steam locomotives on an underground railway line.

The initial route, constructed by the cut and cover method, was almost entirely beneath roadways. It was not until 1890 that technology would allow machines to tunnel beneath the ground deep enough not to affect buildings, but even so, tube companies tended to dig under main highways for safety.

The promoters had to withstand a certain amount of criticism – especially from those whose businesses were disrupted while roads were closed and dug up. There were also some gloomy predictions. *The Times* expressed the opinion that such a line could never be made to pay and added that it was, 'an insult to common sense to suppose that people would ever prefer to be driven amid palpable darkness through the foul subsoil of London'. In 1861 a Dr Cuming opined that 'The forthcoming end of the world would be hastened by the construction of underground railways burrowing into the infernal regions and thereby disturbing the Devil'.

There was some justification in these two comments, for the company had problems dealing with the steam in the tunnels. There was of course only elementary lighting, and journeys in near darkness in the smoke must have seemed a formidable challenge to the nervous. A special locomotive known as 'Fowler's Ghost' was designed intended to consume its own steam but in practice it failed to do so. Daniel Gooch, the Locomotive Superintendent of the Great Western built a class of engine fitted with condensing gear that largely solved the problem of the steam. Even his efforts, however, could do little about the black smoke from the coal furnace. Some parts of the line were open to the elements, in which case the smoke could escape, and along the main road there were also vents, but those parts of the line that were enclosed were wreathed in a noxious, clinging, acrid vapour conducive of sore eyes and sore chests. The problems created by steam locomotives were only overcome when the line was electrified around 1900.

Baker Street station was important to the Metropolitan Railway, for it was from there that the company extended its services as far as rural Middlesex and Buckinghamshire into what John Betjeman would call 'Metroland'.

Great Portland Street station was opened as 'Portland Road'. Its name boards claimed that it served 'Regent's Park East and Zoological Gardens': as the entrance to the latter was almost a mile away, we can either chuckle at the claim or conclude that in a different century people expected to walk longer distances and were fit enough to do so.

Another Metropolitan station, just within the remit of this book, was opened on 13 April 1868. This was St John's Wood Road station on the Metropolitan Line branch from Baker Street which at that time went no further than Swiss Cottage. This station, just south of St John's Wood Road, was eventually renamed Lords in June 1939 but closed five months later when St John's Wood on what is now the Jubilee Line was opened. When Test Matches were played the railway even had a booking office in Lord's.

Marylebone tube station on the Bakerloo Line was first named 'Great Central' when it opened on 27 March 1907 as a temporary terminus while the Bakerloo was being extended west and northwards from Baker Street. At street level, the stations on this line had the distinctive ox-blood red faience tiling introduced by Leslie Green. One panel of tiling bearing the name 'Great Central' can still be seen at platform level but the buildings at street level at the junction of Harewood Gardens and Harewood Row have gone. The passages and staircases below ground still display the cream and green-trimmed tiling of the 1907 era.

MAIL RAIL

Beneath Marylebone was the little known Post Office Railway which opened on 3 December 1927, operating from the Paddington Sorting Office (under the mainline station) running on subterranean track and terminating at Whitechapel. Originally there were seven intermediate stops beneath important postal buildings including Bird Street, Wimpole Street and Rathbone Place. There were later only stops at Paddington, Rathbone, Mount Pleasant and Whitechapel. From Paddington, the train ran roughly beneath Oxford Street and New Oxford Street and then turned north-east to the Mount Pleasant Sorting Office then south and east via the King Edward Building Post Office near Holborn Viaduct, terminating at the Eastern District Post Office in Whitechapel Road. The trains were electric, remotely controlled and ran 80 feet below the surface.

Built initially to reduce road congestion, the Royal Mail decided to close it for reasons of cost on 31 May 2003.[1] Now, the post which the railway satisfactorily carried for over 60 years underground, goes by road.

75. *Marylebone Station, c.1905.*

THE GREAT CENTRAL AND ITS HOTEL

When filmmakers want a station with an atmosphere redolent of Victorian or Edwardian railway travel, Marylebone Station is often their choice. This is London's most picturesque terminus, tucked away in Melcombe Square just to the north of the Marylebone Road, behind the grand (and restored) Edwardian hotel, now called the Landmark. It is the only one of London's long-distance main line termini which was never expanded.

That the station exists is due in part to the energy and vision of one of the great Victorian railway magnates, Sir Edward Watkin (1819-1901). He had interests in many railway companies and effective control of several. One of these was the Manchester, Sheffield & Lincolnshire Railway whose operations, specialising in the movement of coal, were largely spread in a band between Grimsby, Sheffield and Lancashire. He decided as early as the 1860s it would be profitable to extend it southwards through Nottingham, Leicester and Rugby to London. The MS & L R (often called the 'Money, Sunk and Lost'), was not a rich company and it took Watkin until 1893 to obtain parliamentary authorisation for his extension to the capital. In 1897, he renamed the company the 'Great Central Railway'. The extension was but part – albeit a necessary part – of a scheme for a high speed main line from the West Riding of Yorkshire and the East Midlands to London and then via the South Eastern Railway and a Channel Tunnel, in both of which he had an interest, to Paris and other European capital cities.

His proposal that the London terminus should be close to Marylebone Road was resisted by wealthy and influential residents of St John's Wood through which the line would pass. It also generated potent objections from members of the Marylebone Cricket Club who perceived a threat to Lord's cricket ground. His first parliamentary bill, presented in 1891, failed to win the necessary support. Watkin realised that he had under-estimated the influence of the members of the MCC. However, he obtained sufficient funds from the directors of the Company to buy the land and the MCC was also propitiated. Where the railway line passed through the St John's Wood district it was to be in tunnels or covered ways. In March 1893, the Act authorising the Great Central Railway became law.

Once the land had been bought and the line built there was little capital to build the terminus. The company made do with erecting what we see today and very pleasant it is too. Land was acquired for a total of ten platforms but only four were built, or needed. Of the route to the Continent nothing more was heard.

The station opened to the public on 15 March 1899 and the first train departed from Marylebone with four passengers on board.

Slow but comfortable trains left Marylebone for the cities of the East Midlands, for the West Riding and for Manchester, but the Great Central was a latecomer on the railway scene and at a disadvantage. After the nationalisation of the railways in 1948 the longer-distance services out of Marylebone were reduced and then withdrawn. At one point, the station was to be closed, the services to be diverted to other termini. One suggestion involved converting the line into Marylebone to a road serving a coach station to be built on the site. Happily, Marylebone station survives, having been updated. More passengers now than at any previous time use it, travelling on diesel trains into the Chilterns and beyond.

The frontage of the station is formed by a glass porte cochère, part of which stretches across Melcombe Square to provide covered access to the red brick and terracotta hotel, originally called the Great Central. The intention was that the company would own and operate this palatial building but in the event it was financed and built independently. Designed in an Edwardian version of the Jacobean style by an experienced architect, Robert William Edis (1839-1927), it dominated the station. Edis had previously designed a wing of Sandringham, the Constitutional Club in Northumberland Avenue and alterations to Liverpool Street Station Hotel (1901). Characterised by ornament in buff terracotta, with steep gables and a tower,

over the main entrance is a terracotta bas relief of two women, one helmeted with a chestplate of iron, the other déshabillé.

The hotel opened on 1 July 1899. It had 700 bedrooms, a palm court and, allegedly,[2] a cycle track on the roof. In 1916 the hotel was requisitioned by the government for use as a convalescent home and it was requisitioned again during the last war. For many years, as with the Midland Grand at St Pancras, it was used as offices by a number of nationalised transport concerns. In 1993, two years after the refurbishment and re-opening of the Langham *(see p. 63)* the Great Central Hotel also underwent a substantial renovation, reopening as the Landmark. The inner courtyard, sporting fully grown palms and covered by a glass canopy, is impressive.

[1] The Communication Workers' Union claimed that the issue of expense derived from the deliberate policy of running the system down and using it at less than capacity.

[2] The authors, Erica McDonald and David Smith of *Pineapples & Pantomimes* (1992), state that although intriguing, there is no evidence of this.

Pill Island

London, in common with other great cities of ancient origin, has areas devoted to a particular profession or related tradespeople. The Harley Street area is a famous example of this phenomenon. The road runs due north from Cavendish Square to Marylebone Road and was planned in 1729.

Harley Street, bears the name of Edward Harley, 2nd Earl of Oxford and Mortimer, whose role and particularly that of his experienced uncle, also Edward Harley, is described in pp 17-21. It was originally developed as an abode for the fashionable and rich. Richard Rush, US Envoy from 1817 to 1825, described the district as so quiet and the houses so good that it was a favoured place for ambassadors' residences. He said that the houses could be rented from 400 to 1,000 guineas a year; he visited several describing the stone staircases and the carpeted floors and libraries.[1]

At first, Harley Street was divided into Harley Street and Upper Harley Street, numbered consecutively starting on the east side to Weymouth Street. It was renumbered in 1824 and again, definitively, when Upper Harley Street became part of Harley Street in 1864. This re-numbering is a trap for the unwary looking for the home of a former resident.[2] The change from residences to practising rooms for consultants did not begin until the mid-19th century.

Residents first arrived in 1752 – by then Cavendish Square, Wimpole Street and Devonshire Place had already been constructed. Early residents included officers of the armed forces, such as Admiral Lord Keith (1746-1823), Admiral Hood (1724-1816) and the Earl of Mulgrave (1793-1831) military adviser to William Pitt, the Younger. Sir Arthur Wellesley (1769-1852) (later the Duke of Wellington) rented a Harley Street house in 1808 for his wife Kitty and two children when he left for Portugal, and he continued to rent it until 1814, two years before he went to the grandeur of Apsley House.

It is not thought, however, that Wellesley himself lived in the Harley Street house.[3]

Dr. William Rowley, an army surgeon, lived (1760-65) at what was then no. 66 (now 47), but this was well before the area had become associated with medical practice. Dr Thomas Young, known today as a scientist and the author of a theory of colour vision, was a practising physician and lived at No. 48 Welbeck Street from 1799 to 1826, but he was a 'society man' and he lived in Harley Street for its fashionable address.[4]

THE FIGHT FOR PROFESSIONAL STATUS

The history of medical practice has been marked by conflict among its practitioners about professional status, their legal rights and the implementation of new practices and treatments, not to mention the place of women, both as patients and potential practitioners. The claims relating to status and qualifications gave rise to numerous organisations many of which started and are based in Marylebone.

Until 1745, barbers and surgeons belonged to the same company – the Barber-Surgeons – but in that year the surgeons formed the separate Company of Surgeons, which later became the Royal College of Surgeons. The term surgeon described a person who performed operations with the use of surgical instruments. Both apothecaries and surgeons were required to serve an apprenticeship later supplemented by attendance at a school of anatomy.[5] In the 18th and 19th centuries, apothecaries might – as well – prescribe and dispense medicines, but they were distinct from physicians who were trained to diagnose internal disorders and were often educated at Oxford or Cambridge.

THE MEDICAL MEN COME TO HARLEY STREET

By the middle of the 19th century, 'Harley Street' (used in a generic sense to include Wimpole Street, Upper Wimpole Street, Devonshire Place, Welbeck Street, Queen Anne Street, Cavendish Square and Mansfield Place) came to be regarded as the headquarters of doctors known by their experience in a particular field as consultants. As doctors were not permitted to advertise, they needed another 'association' by which to announce to potential clients their qualifications, and an address close to Cavendish Square came to be regarded as a prerequisite. Evidence of this lies in the story told to Percy Flemming, author of *Harley Street*, by Sir John Tweedy. Up to 1888, Sir John had practised at 24 Harley Street close to Cavendish Square. In 1886, he moved to No. 100, between Weymouth and Devonshire Streets, about 500 metres from the Square. On hearing of this move, some of his older colleagues warned him that his practice would suffer.

Before Harley Street became the centre for medical specialists, there had been two earlier enclaves, a small one based on St. George's Hospital in the Piccadilly area and a larger one in the City based on the four hospitals St. Bartholomew's, St. Thomas's, Guy's and the London. Finsbury Square and Circus, Broad Street and Bridge Street were the places of residence.[6]

It is likely that the medical profession moved west following their patients: the rich and fashionable. Additionally, the Marylebone premises and their central location with access to nearly all major train stations were attractions. The number of medical practices in the area grew from about a dozen in the 1860s to over 1500 by 2006.[7] By the 1930s, this south-eastern part of Marylebone became known as Pill Island.

The presence of medical consultants is underpinned by the nearness of substantial independent hospitals. The King Edward VII Hospital was founded in 1899 by two sisters, Agnes and Fanny Keyser, who turned their home at 17 Grosvenor Crescent into a hospital for the care of wounded officers returning from the Boer War. Edward VII was its first patron. The hospital moved to its present site in Beaumont Street in 1948 and in 2000 was renamed King Edward VII Hospital Sister Agnes. In 1932 the London Clinic was established between Harley Street and Devonshire Place. The Portland Hospital which serves only women and children, is at 205-209 Great Portland Street.

MEDICAL ASSOCIATIONS

At Nos. 10a to 12 Chandos Street is a long low stuccoed house two storeys high, built *c.* 1808. It is occupied today by the Medical Society of London, which may be the oldest medical society in the world. It was founded in 1773 by a Quaker physician, Dr John Coakley Lettsom. It sought to bring together the three competing medical practitioners: physicians, surgeons and apothecaries.

Further east is Chandos House (see p. 22), which was designed by Robert and James Adam in 1769-71. This now houses the Royal Society of Medicine, founded in May 1805 as the Medical and Chirurgical Society of London when leading members of the Medical Society of London split to form a new society that would bring together branches of the medical profession 'for the benefit of conversation on professional subjects, for the reception of communications and for the formation of a library'. Nowadays the main office of the Society is at 1 Wimpole Street.

The British Dental Association (founded 1879) is the professional association and trade union of registered practitioners of dentistry. It is at No. 64 Wimpole Street, where there is also a dentistry museum. Dentists were not originally considered to be worthy of professional status. However, a Dentistry Act of 1878 finally established the Association and provided for the regulation of dentistry and its practitioners.

The premises of the Royal College of Nursing in Henrietta Place on the south-west corner of Cavendish Square were bought from Lord Asquith the Prime Minister and have been subsequently expanded. Other organisations in the area include the Royal College of Midwives (Mansfield Street since 1957) and the Royal College of Radiologists (Portland Place); the General Medical Council, established in 1858 to regulate the medical profession, has been in Hallam Street since 1922. The Royal College of Physicians was established in 1518 by Thomas Linacre. It moved to its modern headquarters, designed by Denys Lasdun in 1964, having been in Trafalgar Square for many years.

76. The Medical Society of London headquarters in Chandos Street.

PHARMACIES

At number 105a Crawford Street, the pharmacy Meatier, Higgins and Thomas was established in 1814 (its premises and façade survive), despatching prescriptions all over the world, particularly to explorers and officers serving overseas. The pharmacy John Bell & Croyden was established in 1798 at 50-54 Wigmore Street; it was refurbished and updated in the 1990s.

FAMOUS NAMES IN MEDICINE

Dr Eldridge Spratt (1872-1940) founded the National Hospital for Diseases of the Heart and Paralysis, originally in Margaret Street, in 1857. It is now at 16 Westmorland Street, where the first heart transplant in Britain was undertaken in 1968. The Heart Hospital, as it is now called, previously an independent, was bought by the National Health Service in 2001 so as to speed up the treatment of heart patients.

Dr Edward Bach practised from Harley Street in the 1920s as a specialist in vaccines. In 1892,

Sir Morell Mackenzie, whose consulting rooms were in Harley Street, was one of the first people to suggest a link between smoking and lung cancer. Sir Frederick Treves (1853-1923), at 6 Wimpole Street between 1886 to 1907, published in 1884, *Surgical Applied Anatomy* and was appointed consulting surgeon in 1898 at the London Hospital. Among his most famous patients were King Edward VII and Joseph Merrick, the 'Elephant Man'.

Elizabeth Garrett Anderson (1836-1917), the first English woman to qualify in medicine, established St Mary's Dispensary for Women in 1866 staffed by women. Renamed the New Hospital for Women, in 1872 it moved to Marylebone Road to provide poor women and children with treatment from qualified female doctors.

Florence Nightingale (1820-1910) is regarded as the founder of modern nursing and a rigorous observance of antiseptic practice. After a year of unpaid duties in a London 'Institution for the Care of Sick Gentlewomen' she left for the

77. Joseph Lister.

Crimean War, where she established her first reputation. The Institution was at what is now 90 Harley Street and there is an engraved inscription to her on the building there.

Mary Seacole (1805-1881) also served in the Crimea. She was a Jamaican nurse who lived in a building on the site of what are now George Street Mansions. Born as Mary Jane Grant in Kingston, Jamaica in 1805, her father was a Scots soldier, and her mother a Jamaican from whom she learned her nursing skills. In 1836, Mary married Edwin Seacole, who died in 1844. In 1854, she came to England and asked the War Office if she could be sent as an army nurse to the Crimea. Although this offer was refused, Mary funded her own trip and established the British Hotel near Balaclava to provide 'a mess-table and comfortable quarters for sick and convalescent officers'.

She returned to England after the war destitute and in ill health. In July 1857 a charitable festival was organised to raise money for her. In the same year she published her memoirs, *The Wonderful Adventures of Mrs Seacole in Many Lands*.

Joseph Lister (1827-1912), whose headquarters was at Park Crescent, was Professor of Clinical Surgery at King's College from 1877 to 1893. He introduced the practice of antisepsis, which reduced mortality rates following invasive surgery. He has an established place in the Pantheon of medical pioneers. His statue overlooks the north end of Portland Place.

Sir Henry Thompson (1820-1904) who lived at No. 35 Wimpole Street, trained at University College, London. He became a surgeon and specialist in treatment of diseases of the genito-urinary tract, particularly in the bladder. In 1874, he took a foremost part in founding the Cremation Society of England. Thompson became an enthusiastic spokesman for cremation as a 'necessary sanitary precaution against the propagation of disease'. He was also a gifted amateur artist and, as well, an astronomer.

A FAMOUS QUACK

It is not surprising that the area attracted such a one as John St John Long. He practised in 1828 at number 41 (now 84) Harley Street. He became known as the 'King of Quacks'.

In August 1830, a wealthy woman named Cashin and her two daughters came to London from Dublin in the hope of finding a cure for the consumptive daughter. St. John Long's treatment involved creating an external wound. The wound became gangrenous and the girl died.

At the inquest, witnesses to the treatment testified to its benefits. Nevertheless, Long was charged with manslaughter and committed to Newgate. He was also fined two hundred and fifty pounds.

[1] Percy Flemming, *Harley Street from early times to the present day* (1939), 22.

[2] Richard Bowden, Archivist at the Howard de Walden Estate kindly supplied a diagram of the original numbering and two subsequent renumberings of this street.

[3] Flemming, *op cit*, 20.

[4] *Ibid*, 21.

[5] Nick Black, *Walking London's Medical History (2006)*.

[6] Flemming, *op cit*, 28.

[7] Black , *op cit.*

Fitzrovia

Fitzrovia is a quarter of central London bordered on the east by the Bedford Estate and on the west by the Portland Estate. In his evocative short history of the area,[1] Nick Bailey concentrated on the portion of Fitzrovia which lies in the modern borough of Camden that is east from Cleveland Street to Tottenham Court Road, thereby including Fitzroy Square.

Mainly focusing on the Marylebone part of Fitzrovia, this chapter deals with the area bounded by Oxford Street in the south, Great Portland Street in the west, the Euston Road in the north and in the east by Cleveland Street, Charlotte Street and Rathbone Place.

The number of artists of all kinds living in the area in the 19th century probably indicates that they settled near to their potential clients to the west, in properties that were cheap to rent. This particularly applied to Newman Street and Charlotte Street. But, the term 'Fitzrovia' is modern, coming into use in the 1940s. Partly because of the proximity of the Slade School of Art (est. 1871) in Gower Street, the area flowered again in the '20s and '30s, housing and entertaining artists and art students. Writers congregated as well, especially at the Fitzroy Tavern (on the corner of Charlotte Street and Windmill Street) and other local pubs including the Wheatsheaf at No. 25 Rathbone Place.

78.   Detail from John Rocque's map of 1746, showing the mainly rural nature of the Fitzrovia area. (Reproduced from the facsimile map published by the London Topographical Society in 1982.)

Part of the area was previously called 'North Soho' which reflects its rakish reputation. E.B. Chancellor referred to the eastern part as 'London's Old Latin Quarter'.

EARLY DAYS

John Roque's map of 1746 reveals few buildings in the area, though substantial and prestigious residential development had already taken place to the west including Margaret Street, Mortimer Street and Little Portland Street. The rest consisted of pasture, smallholdings, a timber yard, windmill, some rough ground and a few ponds. The Marylebone manor house could be seen in the mid-distance. A public house called the Adam and Eve lay just west of Wells Street. Nearby lay the Boarded House at which, between 1719 and 1730, the prize-fighter Figg attracted a varied clientele to watch boxing matches – including those between women, which were popular.

In its western reaches, Fitzrovia attracted some affluent residents, creating a need for domestic help and other trades such as piano-makers, plumbers, dressmakers, picture-framers, confectioners and French polishers. Eventually, many of the grander residences fell on hard times and were subdivided into flats or rooms, with consequential neglect of the common areas and frontages. Much of the north of Fitzrovia in the Great Portland and Cleveland Street areas declined into lodging houses, brothels and taverns next door to light industry. Now, many small companies in the service sector have their base in Fitzrovia.

Charles Booth's Poverty map of 1898 identified areas of particular deprivation in Rathbone Street, Riding House Street, Charlotte Mews and Adam and Eve Court. The inhabitants of other streets in the district were largely unskilled and sporadically employed.

A COSMOPOLITAN QUARTER

Enterprising immigrants with skills in catering and cuisine found London a place where they could make a living as restaurateurs. Pagani's at No. 42 Great Portland Street (destroyed in the

79. *A menu cover at Pagani's in Great Portland Street, c.1925. The famous Artists' Room is bottom right.*

2nd World War), was opened by a Swiss-Italian, Mario Pagani, in 1871. His restaurant had an upper façade which had mosaic designed in an art nouveau style by A. Beresford Pite in 1901, and a lower floor created in 1874 by Charles Worley. Its reputation was enhanced by its famous Artists' Room, in which Pagani flattered certain of his clientele by reserving it for their exclusive use.

'At no more than 8 feet square and with space for only one table it was small. But it was reserved for the owner's special guests and from 1874 they had been encouraged to sign their names, sometimes with a message or a caricature, on the brown wallpaper. By the 1890s these signatures, drawings and caricatures, amountng to some 5000, had been mounted onto panels which were interspersed with portraits of the relevant well-known artists, composers, authors, singers, actors and actresses.

Thirteen of the original fourteen panels containing over 5000 signatures still survive, having been removed from the walls for safe-keeping in 1939. They range from Bernhardt to Whistler.[12]

Informal eateries made congenial meeting places for the district's artists. Bertorelli's, opened in 1912 by four brothers, Italian Jews, was at 19 to 23 Charlotte Street. Through the 1930s and the 1940s it became a rendezvous of John Berger, Christopher Isherwood, Hugh Thomas, A.J.Ayer, Stephen Spender, T.S. Eliot, Kingsley Amis and Anthony Powell. In the early '80s, publishing editors (among them, James Cochrane, Paul Sidey and Charles Clark, to name a few) and authors from nearby publishing houses – Hutchinson, then off Fitzroy Square, and Routledge & Kegan Paul, in Goodge Street, lunched there. Guiseppe Bertorelli was its mainstay until his death in 1994 at the age of 101.

In more recent years, notwithstanding the insensitive rebuilding after the bomb damage of the last war, the area has seen a revival of smaller art oriented businesses, bespoke tailoring and specialist suppliers joined by advertising agencies.

THE FITZROY TAVERN AND THE WHEATSHEAF

Two pubs were the haunt of the liveliest of Fitzrovia's drinkers and residents – the Fitzroy and the Wheatsheaf. The Tavern was taken over in 1919 by the personable and hospitable Judah Morris Kleinfeld (1864-1947), who had come from Poland much earlier and who had become naturalised in 1904. He got special dispensation for his bright and educated, but underage daughter Annie (then only 14), to assist him. The business was continued after her father's retirement by Annie and her husband Charles Allchild (1907-88) until their own retirement in 1956.

The Fitzroy became the congenial and welcoming local for many artists, poets and writers, including those from the Omega Workshops and Augustus John. In *Living Up West* by Gerry Black (1994), the author credits the artist Nina Hamnett, who lived locally in Charlotte Street, with first introducing the tavern to her wide acquaintance of artists and writers. The Fitzroy under Allchild was also a meeting place for gays and as Mike Pentelow and Marsha Rowe tell us in their excellent book, *Characters of Fitzrovia* (2001) the police moved in in 1955 and prosecuted Allchild for running a 'disorderly house' and, that old cliché, 'a den of vice'. The police gave evidence that the number of prostitutes and homosexuals in the pub was between 50 and 80 and that some paraded themselves with 'rouged' cheeks and 'blatantly dyed' hair. Despite court-room support from eminently respectable people such as the broadcaster Wynford Vaughan-Thomas and barrister Geoffrey Bing, Allchild was found guilty on nine counts and he was also suspended by the pub's brewery. The verdicts were later overturned, but Allchild resigned anyway, disgusted at the behaviour of the brewery.

The police were more successful at the Wheatsheaf where it persuaded the tolerant landlord not to admit Quentin Crisp. The Wheatsheaf however did play host to the spy Guy Burgess and to George Orwell.

Two of the most notorious Fitzrovian drinkers were Dylan Thomas and the playright Brendan Behan. Thomas usually began his day at the Stag's Head in New Cavendish Street. He was well known in the Wheatsheaf and the famous story is that it was at this pub that he pinched his future wife, Caitlin, from Augustus John one evening in April 1936, and spent the next five nights with her. Thomas, a renowned drunk, was even thrown out of the Rathbone Arts Club at 28 Rathbone Place for his behaviour.

Thomas and Caitlin sometimes lived at 8 Conway Street, a rooming house that also accommodated the poet Roy Campbell and his wife.

80. Theodore Hook.

NAME CHANGES

A number of streets in Fitzrovia have had their names changed. There were two Charlotte Streets – the more famous one, in Camden, retains its old name, but the Marylebone version since 1868 has been renamed Hallam Street. Mortimer Street used to be Charles Street.

BERNERS STREET

No 54 was occupied by a Mrs Tottenham. In 1809, Theodore Hook, a writer and prankster, laid a bet for £1,000 to the effect that he could make an ordinary house in an ordinary street the most famous address in London for a day. Hook contacted tradesmen of every sort ordering goods and services to be delivered to No.54. Promptly the first tradesmen arrived: coalmen with sacks of coal, fishmongers, butchers, bakers, florists, all bearing their wares and jostling to get to the front door. Poor Mrs Tottenham, flustered and embarrassed, turned them away. The prank, known eventually as the Berners Street Hoax, continued throughout the day, until the neighbourhood was in gridlock; the mastermind was the winner of £1,000.

CLEVELAND STREET

Named after the Duchess of Cleveland, the street was originally Upper Newman Street and later Norfolk Street, from Goodge Street to Tottenham Street, and Cleveland Street northwards to the Euston Road. Before development, it was Green Lane, dividing St. Pancras from St. Marylebone and leading to the Green Man on the Euston Road.[3] The borough boundary extended down Cleveland Street (as it still does and crossed Goodge Street between numbers 59 and 61. Cleveland Street is narrow but much used. Most of the houses were built for residential purposes but only No. 120 survives intact. The street's reputation was damaged by the exposure of a gay bordello at No. 19.

No. 19 no longer exists, having been displaced by the Middlesex Hospital (founded 1745). In July 1889, police discovered that Post Office clerks were being procured by the owner, Charles Hammond, for homosexual customers. There was evidence that Lord Arthur Somerset, Lord Euston (the local landowner and the grandson of Queen Victoria), and Prince Albert Victor ('Eddy') were among those involved. Queen Victoria was informed and the Prime Minister Lord Salisbury instituted a cover up. Witnesses and defendants were either allowed to leave or were silenced. The press was hamstrung by the institution of a libel suit.

At No 20 this tale, already shocking, allegedly gets worse. Here was a tobacconist's shop where Annie Elizabeth Crook worked. She lived in the basement of No. 6. In his book, *Jack the Ripper, the Final Solution* (1979) Stephen Knight argues that Prince 'Eddy' had an illegitimate daughter, Alice Margaret, with Annie, whom he then married. The authorities, alarmed because she was both a commoner and Catholic, raided the premises. Poor Annie was committed to a mental institution. Mary Kelly, a witness at their wedding, escaped with the baby girl to the East End, but Mary was later murdered – apparently by Jack the Ripper – in November 1889. The allegation is that the murder was an attempt to ensure that there were no survivors with knowledge of Prince Eddy's conduct.

81. Samuel Morse.

82. Joseph Nollekens, from a painting by Mary Moser.

Charles Dickens' parents took lodgings at No. 22 with a family here (then No. 10 Norfolk Street) when they came to London in 1814. In 1816 they moved up to Camden Town. Dickens returned to live at this house between 1829 and 1831 and then took lodgings at 15 (now 25) Fitzroy Street. Dickens later used 'Green Lanes' (the original name of Cleveland Street) as a setting where the mob took refuge after the Gordon Riots in his novel *Barnaby Rudge*.

Determined to make his name as a painter, Samuel Morse (1791-1872), a native of Massachusetts, came to London in 1811 and lived at 141 Cleveland Street. He received assistance from the painter, Benjamin West, a native of Pennsylvania, who was then President of the Royal Academy. Morse enjoyed several fruitful years, but did not like the noise of a great city. He was, after his return to the US, the inventor of the eponymous Morse Code.

GREAT PORTLAND STREET

Jimi Hendrix (1942-70), an influential instrumentalist who immigrated from the USA and soon became prominent in the London rock music scene, rented a flat near Great Portland Street station in 1966 and was well known in the area.

HALLAM STREET

John Sell Cotman (1782-1842) is recorded as sending paintings to the Royal Academy from what is now Hallam Street (then Charlotte Street) in 1806. The following year so did Cornelius Varley (1781-1873). Dante and Christina Rossetti were both born on the site of 110 (1828 and 1830 respectively), and in Rossetti House at 106 Hallam Street, the writer William Gerhardi (1895-1977) was a resident by 1962. The conductor, Sir Henry Wood (1869-1944), lived at 49 from 1937-39, conveniently near the Queen's Hall.

MORTIMER STREET

At No. 44 (then No. 9) lived the sculptor, Joseph Nollekens (1737-1823), when the road was called Charles Street. His output of work was enormous and at the peak of his success his busts of the famous and titled were much sought after. The famous actor, William Macready (1793-1873), was born in the road, and the writer, Hector

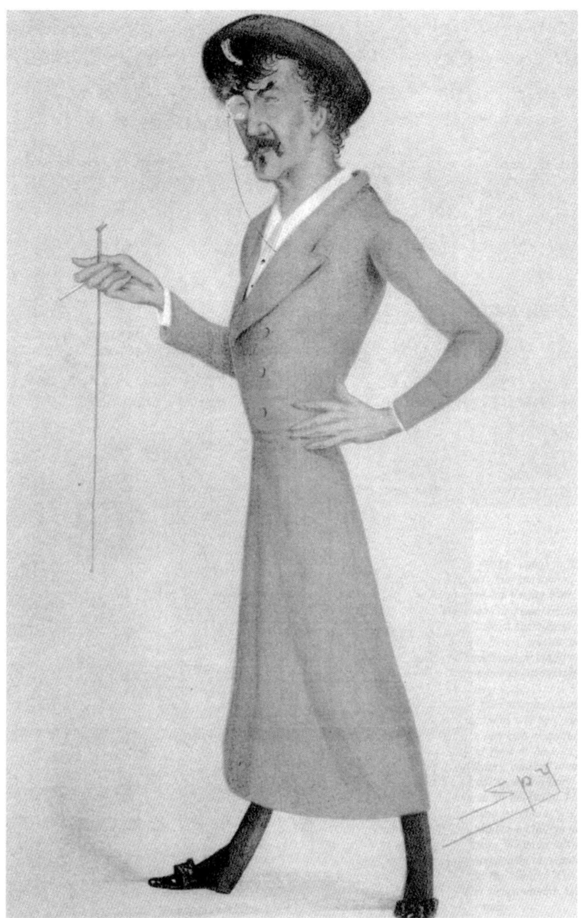

83. A Spy caricature of Whistler in Vanity Fair, *1878. The artist lived in Newman Street for a while.*

Munro (Saki) (1870-1916), lived here from 1909 until his death. The composer, Richard Addinsell (1904-77), was at 25 in the 1940s.

NEWMAN STREET

Numerous artists lived in Newman Street, especially during the 19th century. The most famous was Benjamin West (1738-20) who was at 14 from 1775 until his death. Other residents included the sculptor William Behnes, here from 1818 to 1832, William Dobson 1848-50, Sir Luke Fildes in 1868, William Mulready in 1814 and the illustrator, Sir John Tenniel, in 1837-8. The composer J C Bach was here in 1774, the Kemble family of actors were resident in 1809, and George du Maurier in 1860-61.

James McNeill Whistler (1834-1903), resided for some years at No. 70 with his model and lover Jo Hiffernan until moving to Wapping to be near the Thames.

RATHBONE PLACE

Rathbone Place was developed in the 1720s and the Black Horse pub is recorded by 1746.

William Hazlitt (1778-1830), the essayist and critic, lived at 12 from 1799 to 1803. At No. 17 John Flaxman (1755-1826), lodged as a young man with Mr. Mathew, a cultivated clergyman, who wished to introduce him to society. Flaxman had a long and remarkable career. He was the son of a well known moulder and dealer in plaster casts at the sign of the Golden Head in Covent Garden. For a long period, the son earned his living with the firm of Wedgwood drawing and modelling in low relief on a small scale for jasper ware. In 1800, he was elected to the Royal Academy. Other artists in this street included John Constable (1776-1837) in 1802 and John Linnell (1792-1882) at 35.

At No. 33 John Harris Heal, founder of the furniture firm Heals, set up his bed making and furniture business in 1810. He started as a feather dresser in Leicester Square. In 1818, he moved the business to 203 Tottenham Court Road.

At Nos. 38 and 39, Winsor & Newton, suppliers of artists' materials, opened one of their first shops. Their rivals, George Rowney, were at No. 52.

RIDING HOUSE STREET

At No. 73 lived Olaudah Equiano. Born 1745 in Nigeria, Equiano was kidnapped and taken as a slave to Barbados and between 1757 and 1763 he travelled with his master. In 1766 he purchased his freedom and came to England. He campaigned against slavery, writing in 1789 his life story, *The Interesting Narrative of the Life of Olaudah Equiano or Gustavus Vassa, the African.* He died in 1797 and the house now bears a plaque in his memory.

84. Olaudah Equiano, who lived in Riding House Street.

Liberty's, and well known makers of women's clothing including Jaeger and Jigsaw. Schwenk's also supply theatrical costumiers. The owner, Derek Eddleston has been with the firm since 1990. During the last war, the firm was fined for trading with the occupied Czech Republic and the records of this are still at Schwenk's.

Hand & Lock Embroidery Ltd at 86 Margaret Street specialise in embroidery for military uniforms including metal thread embroidery. They are a fusion of two firms. The first Hand was a Huguenot goldlaceman in 1767 and Stanley Lock in 1956 took over C E Phipps, embroiderers founded in 1898. Hand and Lock merged in 2001.

[1] Nick Bailey, *Fitzrovia* (1981).

[2] Peter Barber and Peter Jacomelli, *Continental Taste: Ticinese emigrants and their Café-Restaurants in Britain 1847-1987* (Camden History Society, 1997), 18.

[3] Bailey, *op cit*.

HABERDASHERY

Wells Street and the surrounding streets have been a centre of trades supporting the haberdashery and clothing industry since the early 19th century. Two examples of this are Schwenk Ltd and Hand & Lock.

Schwenk's at 71 Wells Street was founded by Adolf Schwenk, of German Jewish descent, who had emigrated to Paris from Germany, opening his firm in Paris in about 1900. He began a London branch in 1927, in Dering Street (just south of Oxford Street), moving to Mortimer Street, and then to Newman Street and from there to Wells Street, where the firm has been since 1953 in a building which was previously a choir school. Originally, the firm provided all of the fittings which fashion required, passementerie, braids, laces and buckles of all kinds. The firm supplies the haberdashery departments of the retail trade, such as those at John Lewis and

Oxford Street and its Emporia

Sophie von La Roche, wife of the Councillor to the Elector of Mainz, a writer and sophisticated traveller, who visited London in 1786, commented on Oxford Street:

> 'First one passes a watchmaker's, then a silk or fan store, now a silversmith's, a china or glass shop … just as alluring are the confectioners and fruiterers, where, behind the handsome glass windows, pyramids of pineapples, figs, grapes, oranges and all manner of fruits are on show … most of all we admired a stall with Argand[1] and other lamps, situated in a corner-house, and forming a really dazzling spectacle …
>
> 'Just imagine … a street taking half an hour to cover from end to end, with double rows of brightly shining lamps, in the middle of which stands an equally long row of beautifully lacquered coaches, and on either side of these there is room for two coaches to pass one another; and the pavement, inlaid with flag-stones, can stand six people deep and allows one to gaze at the splendidly lit shop fronts in comfort … Up to eleven o'clock at night there are as many people along this street as at Frankfurt during the fair, not to mention the eternal stream of coaches. The arrangement of the shops in good perspective, with their adjoining living-rooms, makes a very pleasant sight.'

In short, Oxford Street was an affluent shopper's heaven.

The *London Street Views*, 1838 to 1840 published by John Tallis,[2] reproduced in scale the elevations of all the buildings on the important streets of London including Oxford Street. A small sample, from Holles Street (on the north side) to Oxford Circus (then Regent Circus) and continuing east to Wells Street, using the old numbering and running from west to east:

No. 129 Lavenne (from Paris) fancy stationers,
No. 125 Goddards, Chemist, by appointment to the Duchess of Kent
No. 118 at Regent Circus, Blanchards straw Leghorn & millinery warehouse;
No. 103 Peter Robinson

85.   An Ackermann print of 1813, depicting Oxford Street. The view looks west towards the Edgware Road. Stratford Place, with its monumental entrance, is to the right.

Nos. 83, 84 and 85 lace men

No. 82 Nicholay, furrier to Her Majesty,

No. 74 Edward Pattison, ladies' shoe maker (by appointment to Her Majesty)

No. 73 from December 1840 the Princess's Theatre

No. 71 Francis Steele, silversmith, goldsmith and jeweller

There were a myriad other suppliers of every conceivable domestic goods required both for the adornment, furnishing and maintenance of a house.

Despite such consumer attractions, Thomas de Quincey (1785-1859), critic and essayist, nevertheless wrote of Oxford Street, 'stony-hearted stepmother: thou that listenest to the sighs of orphans and drinkest the tears of children'. De Quincey bought his first bottle of laudanum in Oxford Street, the start of his addiction. Thomas Hardy in *Coming up Oxford Street: Evening* describes a City clerk trudging its length, head bowed, eyes fixed on the pavement, asking himself why he had been born.

This chapter deals only with the north (Marylebone) side of the street.

ORIGINS

Oxford Street lies on an ancient route, the Via Trinobantina or Trinovantica, used by the Romans to connect Colchester in Essex to Silchester in Hampshire via the City of London and Staines. The Braun & Hogenberg map of 1560 shows no buildings to the north of the route except the church of Mary-le-Bourne and the manor house of Marylebone. By the 17th century, it was known as 'Tyburn Road' or 'Tyburn Way' but by 1682 it was often referred to as 'the road to Oxford' with variations referring to Uxbridge and Acton and even Worcester. Later maps vary in its name, but usually the 'road to Oxford' is adopted.

John Rocque's map of 1746 shows scattered development along the street. Buildings around the Black Horse, a pub at No. 6 Rathbone Place and its associated yard occupy the eastern boundary at Tottenham Court Road. The Blue Boar was then the easternmost public house on Oxford Street itself. At the eastern boundary Hog Lane went south, a medieval thoroughfare which became part of Charing Cross Road in the 19th century. From Marylebone Lane to Park Lane (then Tyburn Lane) the stretch of Oxford Street is still referred to as Tyburn Road.

At the start of the 18th century, the road was described as 'a deep hollow road and full of sloughs; with here and there a ragged house, the lurking place of cut-throats ...'

During the Civil War in 1643 Parliamentary forces erected fortifications on all the roads leading to the City consisting of both banks and ditches linking forts and gun emplacements. At the east end of Oxford Street near St Giles's Pound, a redoubt was placed near a fort. Other forts were placed at the junctions with Berners Street and Wardour Street. However, these fortifications were never put to the test.

OXFORD STREET COMES OF AGE

In the 1750s the Lords Grosvenor, Portland, Chesterfield, Rockingham and Shrewsbury were among 125 owners of land in Marylebone and Mayfair who petitioned the government that they were "greatly annoyed by the vast concourse of people that always assemble upon days of execution", but hangings at Tyburn did not end until 1783 *(see pp 12-15)*.

By the end of that century, Oxford Street was continuously built up from Tottenham Court Road to Park Lane and Edgware Road.

With the development of Cavendish Square *(see p. 17)* came the planned development of Oxford Market to serve the new and affluent residents north of Oxford Street. The Market, designed by James Gibbs, opened in 1731 to the east of Great Portland Street. It closed in 1876 and was demolished in 1880, but the street names Market Court and Market Place remind us today of its site. Market Street is now Great Titchfield Street.

THE TURNPIKE TRUST

By 1719, five Turnpike Trusts had been established to maintain the great roads leading from London. Oxford Street became a turnpike

86. *The Tyburn turnpike at the western end of Oxford Street, c.1790. The view looks east.*

road in 1721, governed and maintained by trustees in return for the toll income. The trustees included the architect James Gibbs, who lived in Henrietta Street nearby. Gibbs was a friend of the Harleys, and also of William Thomas who as well as being Steward of the Marylebone manor was later the chairman of the trustees.

A tollgate and house were built at the junction with Park Lane; another was at the Tottenham Court Road end. Different rates were levied for carriages, riders, drovers and animals, while prison carts, funerals, mail coaches and soldiers in uniform were generally allowed through for free. At the Tyburn Gate (by Park Lane) in the early 19th century a carriage drawn by one or two horses was charged 10d, a single horseman 4d, and a drover 5d for 20 oxen and 2d for 20 pigs.

COUTURE AND READY-TO-WEAR

By the mid-18th century, as Sophie von La Roche discovered, Oxford Street provided shopping emporia to suit the affluent. From the middle of the next century the small sole proprietor shops tended to amalgamate, becoming partnerships.

The rise of the big department stores of Oxford Street reflects the changes in the social and economic position of women in England. As technology allowed, jobs for women increased dramatically, from telephone exchanges, to retail to typists and clerks. Furthermore, the death of nearly one million British men in the First World War left one million women with the need to earn a living instead of finding a marriage partner.

William Morris noted that London had become, 'The richest city of the richest country of the richest age of the world'.[3] Further, the prosperity meant that,'the social sieve had become decidedly coarser',[4] a waspish metaphor for our more anodyne description of the effects of prosperity on social mobility.

Between 1900 and 1920, the buying of clothing by all women underwent a sea change. Before, fashionable women whose town residences were in Marylebone and Mayfair shopped for fashion, when it was not couture or bespoke, at such places as Marshall & Snelgrove in Oxford Street, Swears and Wells in 1879 in Regent Street, Whiteleys in Bayswater, Dickins & Jones in

87. Victorian shoppers.

Regent Street, and among other places in Kensington, Harvey Nichols.

For couture, Paris dictated style (and did until, perhaps, the mid-1960s). However, some English women of means eschewed Parisian-based style, preferring the English version at the larger houses of, for example, Worth, Redfern, Creed and Lucile[5] and later, notably, Hartnell, Hardy Amies, Molyneux and the quixotic Charles James.

There were also smaller establishments, houses of superior dressmaking and styling skills who followed the leaders, but also had their own style. Among them were Sarah Fullerton Monteith Young[6] and Reville and Rossiter,[7] Madame Hayward, Mascotte,[8] Russell and Allen, Woollands and Wilson, Madam Ross.[9] While the specialist workrooms might well have been in and around Fitzrovia, the retail premises of these smaller establishments were by and large in Mayfair, closer to their clientele.

The shift from couture to ready-to-wear happened quickly, the result of the availability of mass production of patterns and their publication, new fabrics (in particular rayon and knits) and last, but not least, that increasingly even affluent women led lives requiring hard-wearing fabrics which could be cleaned easily, no matter how elegant. Coco Chanel led the way in this, inspired by upper-class Englishmen's sports wear[10] and then moving into easy knitted fabrics.

The copying of this 'modern' style was the strength of the department stores. They displayed under one roof, for women of various levels of affluence, thousands of articles of clothing, which one could buy and take home on the same day. The First World War and the later prolonged economic depression affected all luxury trades, including couture. Many enterprises such as Marshall & Snelgrove amalgamated or closed.

However, the *Post Office London Directory* of 1928 reveals many small businesses in Oxford Street still selling either custom-made, bespoke or ready-made goods including boots, shoes, dresses, furs, hats, mourning clothing, silver, china and providing as well, innumerable services such as accountancy, surveying and banking.

A BUS RIDE

A number of larger shops came to dominate and indeed to denote Oxford Street. These are described in this imaginary ride going west from Tottenham Court Road on top of a bus, looking at the shops and other premises on the north – Marylebone – side of the road. Often there is much of architectural interest above street level, but lower than that not much of distinction.

Originally, the numbering of Oxford Street was consecutive from Tottenham Court Road in the east to Park Lane in the west on the north side, crossing over and then continuing consecutively from west to east down the south side. This was altered in 1880.

No. 6, The Tottenham. The present 1892 building is by Saville & Martin. There was a tavern on the site from 1790 which from 1826 to 1894 was called the Flying Horse. The plaque on the front indicates that it is linked to an alleyway called Boziers Court, which is also shown on Tallis' *London Street Views*, Part 40. The interior of this pub is rare: theatrical ceiling paintings of the Seasons by Felix de Jong & Co and painted mirrors.

Nos 14-16 are on the site of a coaching inn called the Boar & Castle. That was supplanted by the Oxford Music Hall, which opened in March 1861. Altogether there were four different theatre buildings, the last one demolished in 1927/8. It was rebuilt as a Lyons restaurant, one of the early chains of fast food suppliers. Joseph Lyons & Co. was formed from the partnership of Salmon & Gluckstein[11] (which is shown on the 1928 directory at No. 12), a tobacconist chain with two premises on Oxford Street. Salmon and Gluckstein were from established Anglo-Jewish families, part of what is known as The Cousinage or The Family, closely-knit families mostly of Sephardic origin who had arrived early in the 18th century. Lyons had numerous outlets on both sides of Oxford Street.

Nos. 116 to 132 were the premises of **Bourne & Hollingsworth**. Messrs Bourne and Hollingsworth commenced business in 1894, moving to Oxford Street in 1902 to escape the competition of Whiteleys in Westbourne Road. Previously on this site had been 33 businesses which included a tailor, lace merchant, pub, dairy, barber, coffee house, carpet layer and a group of Polish tailors. The site was redeveloped in the Art Deco style 1925/7 by Slater & Moberly. Bourne & Hollingsworth brought to Oxford Street more of the lower or general trade, which the dealers in 'high end' goods deplored. In 1985, the site was redeveloped, retaining the façade and there has been a further refurbishment 1996/8 by the Colman Partnership. A distinguishing feature is a winged female figure by Michael Rizzello, (1997) affixed to the façade, leaning out over Oxford Street.

Nos. 142-144 (previously Francis Steele, silver and goldsmith and jeweller) were the premises of **Jay Richard Attenborough**, diamond merchants and goldsmiths. At the time of writing the building is boarded up and advertised as 'important retail premises for lease'. Attenborough also operated a pawnbroking

88. Jay Richard Attenborough's in Oxford Street.

89. The Waring and Gillow shop.

VISITORS TO LONDON who seek to be corseted in the very latest mode are cordially invited to avail themselves of the services of our Expert Fitters in order to assure that latest touch which gives the outer garments their character and distinctiveness. A fitter will be sent to your hotel with a selection of the celebrated Bon Ton or Royal Worcester Kidfitting Corsets upon request by telephone or post.

AMERICAN LADIES will find in our Corset Showrooms a full range of the newest models of Bon Ton Corsets, which are, by special arrangement, shown here simultaneously with the first exhibits in New York, Paris and Vienna.

PETER ROBINSON'S, OXFORD STREET, LONDON, W.
Telephone: GERRARD 8512.

90. Advertisement for Peter Robinson, early 20th century.

service around the corner in Adam and Eve Court. Here, in 1910, Hawley Harvey Crippen, pawned for £195 the jewellery of his murdered wife before he attempted to flee to Canada with his mistress.

Nos. 156 to 162 on the corner of Winsley Street, was Mappin House, silversmiths. Jonathan Mappin, had been a cutler in Sheffield. The firm had premises on the south side of Poultry in 1870 and the Oxford Street branch opened in 1906. The building was designed by Belcher and Joass, at which the architect A. Beresford Pite *(see p. 28)* worked for some years. Cherry & Pevsner identify the inspiration for the design as Michelangelo of San Lorenzo (in Florence). New premises were built for Mappin by J.J. Joass in 1915 at No.172 Regent Street. The building in Oxford Street has dormers and a Portland stone frontage.

Between Winsley Street and Wells Street was the Queen's Bazaar which, in the 1830s, was aimed at a rich female clientele, but at the time of Tallis's View (1838-40) No. 73 is identified as a Cane and Oil Warehouse. In December 1840 the Princess's Theatre *(see p. 123)* opened on the site.

Nos. **164-182** were the premises of **Waring & Gillow**, distinguished furniture makers and furnishers. Gillow, a Lancaster firm, originally leased an impressive 5-bay building between Duke and Orchard Streets, now part of the site of Selfridge's. Richard Gillow, one of the three sons of the founder of the firm, devised important innovations in furniture design including the extending dining table. S.J. Waring, also a firm of joiners and furniture makers, merged with Gillow in or about 1897 and in 1906 moved to this site to a building designed by R. Frank Atkinson in 1901. Professor Charles Reilly in *London Streets and Recent Buildings* (1922) described it as "Wren's east wing of Hampton Court on stilts". That will do admirably and very handsome it is too. Atkinson, who was also involved in the design of Selfridge's, had collaborated with Norman Shaw on the Royal Insurance Company Building in Liverpool.

At the time of writing the premises, consisting of an island site from Winsley Street to Great Titchfield Street, are being restored. The Portland stone dressings on the returns and the garlanded oval windows down the side streets are glorious.

91. *Peter Robinson's shop at the prominent corner of Oxford Street and the upper part of Regent Street.*

92. Oxford Circus – then called Regent Circus – before the rebuilding of Regent Street.

93. The first premises of John Lewis at what was then No. 132 Oxford Street, depicted in Tallis's Street Views c.1838.

94. John Spedan Lewis.

Waring & Gillow did much custom work for many important London clubs and institutions, including the Reform Club and various hotels such as the Midland Grand at St Pancras. The brand Waring & Gillow survives.

At **214 to 234** to Oxford Circus and around the north-east corner was **Peter Robinson**, high class suppliers of clothing and mourning outfits. Eventually, Peter Robinson became a purveyor of high street down-market women's clothes, but is no longer there.

When Regent Street was constructed in the 1820s, **Oxford Circus** was called Regent Circus. The first façades, designed by John Nash, are shown on Tallis's *Views* and in ill. 92. The present curved façades were designed by Sir Henry Tanner, begun in 1913 and completed over a fifteen-year period.

At **277 to 288** is **John Lewis**. Lewis (1836-1928), was a draper's apprentice who in 1856 worked at Peter Robinson's buying silk. He opened his own business in 1864 as a single frontage at what was then number 132, a four-storey Georgian building *(see ill. 93)*. John Lewis flourished and expanded into neighbouring properties and built his own comprehensive store in 1895 on the same site.

His son, John Spedan Lewis (1885-1963), attended Westminster School, joining the business at nineteen. Spedan was put in charge of Peter Jones in Sloane Square, which his father had also purchased. It was here that Spedan developed his policy of sharing profits with

95. *John Lewis's new building, seen from Cavendish Square, being erected in 1938. It was to be badly damaged by bombing in the Second World War.*

staff. This scheme was extended when Spedan took over all the John Lewis stores, which eventually included John Barnes at Swiss Cottage and Jones Bros. at Holloway. In 1928, he turned the whole group of stores into a profit sharing partnership.

The Oxford Street store was destroyed by bombing in 1940 but a new building was opened on 7 October 1960, designed by Slater and Uren. On the east façade is mounted a commissioned sculpture by Barbara Hepworth (1963), redolent of that period called 'Winged Figure'. The north façade facing Cavendish Square is described in more detail on p. 22. It was designed in 1939 by Slater Moberly & Uren with Franz Singer: this was part of a complete rebuilding planned in 1936 and interrupted by the war.

Nos. 308 to 318 lie between Old Cavendish Street and Chapel Place. Formerly this was **D. H. Evans** and is now The House of Fraser; it was the first department store to be fitted with escalators. The building, by Louis Blanc, dates from 1935 to 1937. It replaced a short-lived neo-Baroque premises by John Murray of 1909. D.H. Evans began at this site in 1879.

At **Nos. 334 to 348** are Debenhams. **Debenham & Freebody** once traded from very grand premises in Wigmore Street, built in 1907. The Debenham drapery business developed from Flint and Clark's drapery, which became Clark & Debenham when William Debenham joined the company. On his death in 1863 the business was run by his son Frank Debenham (1837-1917). By that time the store was called Debenham &

96. *Clark & Debenham's old shop in Wigmore Street.*

97. *Marshall & Snelgrove's grand shop during its heyday.*

98.   The Marshall & Snelgrove shop early 20th century.

Freebody, the latter the maiden name of William's wife.

The real engine of the store's expansion was Frank's son, Ernest (1865-1952), who was also later to acquire Marshall & Snelgrove and Harvey Nichols when both of those stores were in financial trouble.

Their old building in Wigmore Street is now used for corporate purposes.

Debenhams in Oxford Street now occupies the old site of **Marshall & Snelgrove** which itself was a merger in 1838 of businesses owned by James Marshall and John Snelgrove. In 1870 the store, previously a conglomeration of single properties, was redeveloped complete with fish-scale tiled mansard roof, in the 'Second Empire' or 'French Chateau' style by Horace Jones and Octavius Hansard.

By 1888, the firm employed over 2,000 of whom 700 boarded on the premises. This small army worked long hours; there was a staff library, smoking and sitting rooms and other leisure facilities.

The First World War hit the grand firm hard. It merged as we have seen above with Debenham & Freebody, but maintained its own name. The store cultivated an air of exclusivity by maintaining an on-site couture work-room to supplement the ready-to-wear lines. In 1973, all the Marshall and Snelgrove stores became 'Debenhams'. The site was redeveloped in 1968-1971 by Adrian V. Montagu & Partners. There is nothing to recommend the exterior of this building and it does not enhance Oxford Street.

Stratford Place lies at one of the entrances to Bond Street tube station. It was built in 1775 on the site of the Lord Mayor's Banqueting House where he and the Corporation of the City of London would feast after their periodic inspections of the water conduits here which supplied some of the City's water. *(See p. 9)*

The buildings of Stratford Place have had some distinguished residents including Martin van Buren, who later was the eighth President of the

99. *Gordon Selfridge.*

100. *An early advertisement for Selfridge's.*

United States, and Sydney Smith, the essayist and wit. Smith today is perhaps best remembered for saying of Lord Macaulay, the historian that, "He has occasional flashes of silence that make his conversation perfectly delightful."

Dominant of the buildings is Derby House (formerly Stratford House) at its northern end, since 1962 the Oriental Club.

No.362 to 366: was another Lyons restaurant, designed by Lewis Solomon & Son in 1915/16.

Nos. 398-454 are now taken up by **Selfridge's.** This store, which opened in March 1909, provided London with a department store of unprecedented scale and grandeur, though the building, as we know it, was not completed until 1928.

The story of Selfridges is the subject of several

works.[12] Harry Gordon Selfridge (1858-1947) demonstrated his entrepreneurial skills at the department store Marshall Field in Chicago and is credited with introducing many retail techniques, including making stock 'reachable', employing a 'greeter' to welcome and direct customers entering the premises, introducing an annual sale, and the 'bargain basement'. Having failed in his bid to buy Marshall Field, he looked to London, which he regarded as the centre of the trading world but with disappointing stores. He built his store at the unfashionable end of Oxford Street, but at least he had the recently opened Central Line to transport his customers. Before the sensational advent of his store wealthier shoppers would drive in their carriages or cars up Bond Street, turn right into Oxford Street and then south into Regent Street. Things were to change.

Selfridge commissioned initial drawings from Albert D. Millar of Daniel Burnham's Chicago practice. The elevation designs were modified in 1907 by Francis Swalesa, a Canadian, French trained. Selfridge then retained the architect of the recently completed Waring & Gillow building, R. Frank Atkinson. The steel frame on which the building is based was designed by Sven Bylander, a Swede who lived in New York, who had worked on the London Ritz. Steel framed architecture was to transform large commercial premises.[13] Original plans included an enormous dome but this was abandoned because the London Building Act of 1894 stipulated a height restriction of 80 feet.

Selfridge granted the new BBC the right to put its radio masts atop the store. He also hired John Logie Baird to demonstrate his new invention of television.

The entrance consists of two free-standing Ionic columns set in a square stone frame, supporting the parapet. The metalwork surrounding the entrance is bronze. The two outer doors are flanked by two human figures representing Science and Art, designed by Sir William Reid RA. Over the main entrance is a sculpture depicting the Queen of Time. It is 11 feet high, her wings overlaid in gold and her robe inlaid with blue faience mosaic. She stands on a ship's prow. The group was designed by Gilbert Bayes and A. D. Millar and installed in October 1931.

ERSTWHILE EMPORIA

Catchpole & Williams were jewellers at No. 510. Here, the Earl of Strathmore, father of Elizabeth Bowes Lyon, bought his daughter an antique tiara at this shop to commemorate her engagement to the then Duke of York, later King George VI after the abdication of his brother Edward.[14]

Hamley's, the toy shop, now in Regent Street, were at 512-14 Oxford Street. The same applies to **Jaeger's** of Regent Street, who were at 352-4.

WORKING IN THE SHOPS

It was no secret that the working conditions of shop workers were disgraceful and restricted – many of them lived in dormitories belonging to their employers. They worked long hours, sometimes 90 a week. In 1886, the Shop Hours Regulation Act stopped staff under 18 from working more than 74 hours a week. In 1896 the Truck Act prevented employers paying wages in anything but money, and protected staff from unfair fines. In 1912 the Shops Act provided for compulsory and fixed meal times and for a weekly half-day holiday.

Gordon Selfridge was, relatively speaking, enlightened in this regard: by 1930, he employed 15,000 people and the store had guidelines and training operations. John Spedan Lewis, as we have seen, put into practice his view that staff should have a share of the profits and be regarded as 'partners'.

[1] Argand lamps were invented in 1780 by Aime Argand and were a form of oil lamp, which by its more sophisticated mechanism increased the amount of light; they were expensive and new in 1786.

[2] Tallis *London Street Views*, 1838-1840, published in facsimile by the London Topographical Society, second edition, 2002.

[3] Geoffrey Munn, *Tiaras. A History of Splendour* (2001), quoting William Morris, 101.

[4] *Ibid*, quoting J. Mordaunt Crook in his *The Rise of the Nouveaux Riches*, 180

[5] The professional name of Lady Duff Gordon; her business address was 23 Hanover Square.

[6] Mount Street, Mayfair and then later South Audley Street, Mayfair.

[7] Traded under several names including Reville Terry and were court dressmakers to Queen Mary; taken over by Worth in 1936.

[8] 29 Church Street, Kensington

[9] 19 Grafton Street, Mayfair

[10] One of her important supporters (and lovers) was the Duke of Westminster, whose clothes Chanel borrowed.

[11] One of the daughters was the painter Gluck.

[12] Gordon Honeycombe, *Selfridges* (1984) is particularly good.

[13] Alastair Service, *London 1900* (1979), 114

[14] Geoffrey Munn, *op. cit.*

Looking After the Poor

In 1861 the population of Marylebone had risen to 162,000 (from 63,000 in the first official Census of 1801). The social class of those inhabitants were chiefly 'gentry and trades-people and scarcely any manufactures.'[1] However, Marylebone had its poor and homeless together with the associated problems: disease, infanticide and other crime. The local authority and residents struggled to develop institutions to deal with the problems on other than a stop-gap basis.

Nikolaus Pevsner noted that by the mid-19th century 'southern Marylebone had sunk in social esteem and the small courts and alleys behind the main streets and squares became squalid and overcrowded'. Barrett's Court (now St. Christopher's Place, and comprising shops, restaurants and solicitors' offices) exemplified the overcrowded slum areas behind Oxford Street. In the houses there bought in 1872 for the social reformer, Octavia Hill, there were forty-five families in forty-nine rooms. The west side of St. Christopher's Place was rebuilt as five-storey model lodgings to designs by Elijah Hoole.[2]

Near the old Ragged School building in Grotto Passage *(see below)* adjacent to Moxon Street is a blue plaque which marks the site of Paradise Place, where Octavia Hill began her work as a housing reformer in the 1860s. In 1864, John Ruskin bought three houses for £750 in Paradise Street which were described as in 'a dreadful state of dirt and neglect.' He gave them to Octavia Hill to manage with the aim of making 'lives noble, homes happy, and family life good.'

On Charles Booth's 1898 Poverty map of London coloured to show areas of social and economic class in London, black denoted the 'lowest class, vicious, semi-criminal'; dark blue indicated 'very poor, casual, chronic want' and light blue, 'poor, 18s a week for a moderate family' whereas red was 'middle–class well-to-do' and yellow was 'upper middle and upper classes, wealthy'. In south Marylebone, pockets in Lower Berkeley Street, Seymour Mews, Lower Seymour Street, Somerset Street, Orchard Street, Oxford Street, Duke Street and what was Paradise Street (now Moon Street) showed these dark colours existing alongside the much larger areas of reds and yellows.

In 1751, Henry Fielding described the lodging houses affording accommodation to the Irish poor in St Giles-in-the-Fields. In the 19th century, during the first potato blight in Ireland, the Irish came to Lisson Grove, Holloway, Camden Town, Kensal Rise and Marylebone, and in particular to the Calomel Buildings off Orchard Street.

Living conditions were primitive, sanitation rudimentary and overcrowding endemic with members of large families sharing a single room. Cholera,[3] caused by ingesting food or water contaminated with the bacterium, was a problem in London as late as 1865. The first cholera pandemic in Europe occurred from 1829 to 1851. In 1832, 6,536 people died in London. The mortality rate was proportionately high among the poor. Peter Ackroyd's *Biography of London* notes: in 'Orchard Street, Marylebone, there were twenty-three houses, which between them contained seven hundred people together with one hundred pigs creating 'very nauseous smells.''

Some houses around the notorious slum areas of Bolsover and Clipstone Streets were rebuilt around 1900 as blocks of flats. Similar properties were also cleared after 1889 from Moxon Street where model buildings for the working poor were erected known as Ossington Buildings – these still survive.

INFANTICIDE

The rates of death among children younger than one year were very high in the 18th and 19th centuries.[4] A baby born to an unmarried woman was pre-eminently at risk and it was estimated that there were up to 65,000 unwanted children born each year in mid-Victorian Britain. *The Times* reported in 1861 that '[between 1856 and 1861], 278 infants had been murdered in London', and this was a low estimate, reliable statistics being difficult to come by.

In the 1860s the Superintendent Registrar for Marylebone, Dr Bachoffner, found that the death rate of children registered as being born out of wedlock under the age of one, ranged from 46 to 93 per cent in his district. Between 1857 and 1859, the *Marylebone Mercury* reported a number of cases of infant deaths: a corpse of a baby in a basket found by two young men in Regent's Park; a housemaid whilst attending a church service in Manchester Square found a parcel at her feet containing the corpse of a baby; a charwoman cleaning a house in Bryanston Square found a 'bundle' in the loft which was the mummified corpse of a baby. .

The Medical Officer for St Marylebone commented in a report to the parish in 1860 on the 'opprobrium of our parish month by month' regarding the unsolved cases of abandoned babies. *The British Medical Journal* in March 1861 noted that Marylebone and Paddington parishes were 'especially infamous as seats of such massacres of the innocents.'

Marylebone had a concentration of affluent households with many servants and the number of illegitimate births reflected the density of the population and the living conditions of those servants. If a servant became pregnant out of wedlock, discovery meant instant dismissal without references and social opprobrium that few could endure. Therefore, secrecy and quick disposal of the evidence were imperative.

The problem of children born out of wedlock amongst servants was exacerbated by the preference of employers of domestic servants for single people. In William Tayler's *Diary of a Footman* compiled in 1837[5] Mr. Tayler, a liveried footman in the service of a Mrs Prinsep in Great Cumberland Street, kept his own marriage a secret and, as well, the birth of his first child, not even recording it openly in his diary. He wrote only obliquely of his wife, Maria, and his sons, particularly William (junior) born in November 1837. William records for 5 November, "I have had a holiday and have been to a christening, *but to whos I do not say*. Spent a very pleasant day."

The birth certificate of William's son, records him born on 24 September of 1837. On 30 September, William wrote, *"having a particular friend unwell I generally go to see her twice a day, that is before dinner and before supper"*. The editor of the *Diary* speculates that his discretion is due to his concern about his position should it be known that he was both married and a father. This prejudice may have induced, in the desperate, infanticide.

CHILD PROSTITUTION AND SLAVERY

In 1880, William Thomas Stead (1849-1912) moved to London to edit with John Morley the *Pall Mall Gazette*. By 1883, he was acting editor. Stead published a series of articles called *The Maiden Tribute of Modern Babylon* out of which he was imprisoned for two months.

In London, young girls could be bought for a few pounds and employed as child prostitutes in the capital or exported to Europe. Their plight was brought to Stead's attention by Josephine Butler, who campaigned for women's rights and by the Salvation Army. Stead exposed this

101. W. T. Stead.

scandal in the *Pall Mall Gazette* and he set out to establish the truth by 'buying' 13-year-old Eliza Armstrong from her parents in Charles Street,[6] Marylebone for £5. Having purchased her, she was taken to a brothel to await a 'client'. Stead published the story, which was a sensation: sales of the *Pall Mall Gazette* soared. However, Stead's role in the events caused an outcry. Although he went to prison for unlawfully kidnapping a minor, the publicity attending the case led Parliament in 1885 to pass the Criminal Law Amendment Act raising the age of sexual consent from thirteen to sixteen and strengthening legislation to protect children from sexual exploitation.

WAIFS AND STRAYS

In 1617 the Lord Mayor of London gathered all the heads of the vestries of London together to require them to agree that 'waifs and strays' should be gathered off the streets where, he said, they were a menace, and then shipped to the New World – in effect sold into slavery. The vestries agreed. Well into the 20th century this practice, albeit in a different form, continued.

The Waifs and Strays' Society was founded in 1881 by Edward de Montjoie Rudolf (1852-1933), a civil servant. He also worked with his brother, Robert, as a Sunday School teacher, in a poor area of South Lambeth. They identified a need for Church of England Homes for destitute children, which did not require payment for admission. In 1893, the Society's name was the Church of England Incorporated Society for Providing Homes for Waifs and Strays, which evolved into today's Children's Society. In January 1882 a house in Clapton was rented and opened as the first boys' home and in 1883 the Marylebone Home for Girls at 14 Quebec Street became the Society's second home. Certified by the Education Act 1870, the Home was to receive impoverished and orphaned girls already in workhouses. Two years later the Home moved to 123 Marylebone Road, which accommodated thirty girls (aged 7-12). The new location was near Marylebone Central School, which many of the girls attended. In the home after their school work, the girls focused on needlework and laundry, preparing them for work in domestic service.

St Hilda's Home For Girls was established in 1889 in premises at New Street, Dorset Square, and transferred to the Waifs and Strays' Society in 1895. The following year St Hilda's moved to 194 Marylebone Road, accommodating twenty-five girls (aged 6-14), but by 1909 it had closed, and the receiving home, St. Elizabeth's in Clapham Common, housed girls of all ages.

SCHOOLS FOR THE POOR

Nearby, just to the north of Moxon Street through the pedestrian passage, is Grotto Passage which owes its origin to John Castles (?-1757), grotto builder and entrepreneur of the mid-18th century, whose work is described on p. 54. A Ragged School was founded here in 1846 and in 1895 it was known as the Grotto Passage Home for Lads.

The current building retains a sign referring to the Ragged and Industrial Schools 1846. The concept of a 'ragged school' – free education for poor children – was developed by John Pounds, a Portsmouth shoemaker. In 1818 he began teaching poor children without charging fees, and a Thomas Guthrie helped promote Pounds' idea by starting a ragged school in Edinburgh. Lord Shaftesbury formed the Ragged School Union in 1844 which recognised that charity, denominational and so-called dame schools were not providing for the growing numbers of children in poverty in cities.

Other schools for the poor included a Day School of Industry, established in 1791 in Paradise Street for 300 children. Supported by voluntary contributions, charity sermons and the children's earnings – they were employed in plaiting straw and the girls also did needlework. In 1808, Sir Thomas Bernard (1750-1815), a philanthropist, proposed a scheme for the education of the poor of St Marylebone. The aim was to provide children with a useful and religious instruction which would qualify them 'for situations in life'. The school, located in a house and garden in the High Street,

102. St Marylebone Charity School, the main frontage on Marylebone Road.

accommodated 500 children in 1833. There was also a ragged school on Lisson Street in 1854 where girls 'carried out toy work.'

St Marylebone Charity School was first on Marylebone High Street between 1750 to 1838 and then Marylebone Road until 1907. It was founded for 'instructing, clothing, qualifying for useful servants, and apprenticing, the Children of industrious poor Parishioners'. The (by then widowed) Countess of Oxford (1694-1755) gave the trustees a piece of ground in the High Street in 1754 for a term of 999 years at a peppercorn rent. By 1822 the charity clothed, maintained and educated 120 children. The support of wealthy parishioners was essential.

There was also a School of Industry for Female Orphans at Lisson Grove. The St Marylebone Health Society was established in 1906 to deal with high levels of infant mortality in some of the worst slums of Lisson Grove.

MARYLEBONE WORKHOUSE

The Marylebone parish workhouse opened its doors in 1752, a product of the Knatchbull Workhouse Act of 1723 which determined that the system of poor relief should be confined as much as possible to workhouses. The parish had a right to decline relief to those refusing to enter.[7]

Workhouses were intended to be a deterrent to prevent the able-bodied sheltering there, by making the conditions harsh and shameful and by requiring the entire family to enter the workhouse. If this happened, the parents (sometimes only the surviving mother) were separated from the children and allowed only limited access to them. Many poor people would go to extremes to avoid entering a workhouse, but sometimes it was the only alternative to starvation and homelessness.

In 1731 Edward Harley, the 2nd Earl of Oxford (1689-1741), gave land to the south of Paddington Street for use as a burial ground and for the building of almshouses and workhouses. In 1750, after much delay and political wrangling, the construction of a workhouse there began and it came into use in 1752 accommodating about forty inmates. It stood at the north-east corner of the New Burial Ground, facing Paddington Street. But it was hopelessly small and the building which had been erected to take forty had 220 inmates by 1772.[8]

THE NEW WORKHOUSE

The Vestry then acquired land to the north of the burial ground on the south side of Marylebone Road – part of the site belonged to the Duke of Portland and part to Henry Portman. A new workhouse was opened in 1776 in what is now Luxborough Street together with an infirmary built in 1792.

Extensions were added over the years, but by the 1840s demand for places in the workhouse exceeded 2000 and this was increased by those fleeing famine in Ireland. High numbers also brought pressures to economise. St. Marylebone sent its infants to the country in an attempt to improve their dire mortality rates. At the age of six, they were returned and spent the next four to ten years in the Workhouse where the regime was brutal.

In 1867, new building works began which included a new casual ward. The *Illustrated London News* reported that the Marylebone Workhouse was 'in every respect a good example to the other London workhouses [when it] was opened last week for the accommodation of tramps or casual poor; about 11,000 of whom, men, women, and children obtained relief in the last six winter months.'

In 1895, approval was given for the demolition and re-design and replacement of all the remaining buildings built before 1867. A new building was opened in March 1900. Although the population of the workhouse rose above its approved 1,921 inhabitants, this then reduced after the implementation of old age pensions (1908), the establishment of labour exchanges

103. St Marylebone Workhouse Infirmary, built to the north-west of the main building. Watercolour of 1803.

104.   The new ward for the casual poor. From the Illustrated London News, 28 Sep. 1867.

(1909) and the initiation of compulsory insurance against sickness and unemployment (1911). In 1930 the London County Council took over the functions of the 26 Boards of Guardians and the 4 poor law school districts.

At the beginning of the First World War the casual ward block accommodated Belgian refugees and was then used after the war as a military detention barracks. The Marylebone Workhouse, by then a care facility, closed in January 1965, the buildings demolished and replaced by flats and accommodation for the London Polytechnic. The University of Westminster now covers the site.

The residents, mostly elderly, were moved to other more appropriate accommodation, either specialised or smaller.[9]

105. Ranks of men in the Workhouse dining room, eating in silence, pictured in Living London by George Sims (1902.)

HOUSING THE WORKING CLASSES

Numerous charities throughout London in the 19th century built 'artisans' dwellings', most notably the Peabody Trust. Generally they were unattractive, but better than the residents had been used to, and were almost always rented out to the lower paid who had regular employment. It was even more important then that the people who provided services to the metropolis lived near their places of employment.

In Marylebone a good example of such housing is Seymour Buildings. These were constructed in 1889 to 'provide accommodation for the working classes at the lowest possible level'. Built of London stock in 5 or 4 storeys around a courtyard, which is now a garden, the most interesting architectural feature of the flats on the outside are gargoyles at the roofline.

In the mid 1960s, Westminster Council, which had taken over the buildings, moved the tenants to more modern accommodation. The flats, in danger of being demolished, were squatted and in 1975 the squatters secured a licence to remain. They formed the Seymour Housing Co-operative and by 1984, the flats had been re-designed by Kay Jordan, an architect with Solon Co-op Housing Services and they are now a successful example of low-rent inner-city co-operative housing.

The rise in office work, retail and telephone exchanges gave opportunities for work to women previously unavailable. After the 1st World War, because so many young men had died, there were estimated at least one million women in Britain who would not find husbands. They needed work and accommodation. York Street Chambers, built in 1892, was a block of 50 flats for single women: artists, authors, nurses and other working women, with a common dining room and kitchen in the basement.

BLACK AND ASIAN POOR

During the 1780s, Asian seamen (Lascars) employed by the East India Company serving on ships bringing goods from India, were left stranded in London without means of support. Destitute, and in a harsh climate and culture, they resorted to begging on the streets. Concerned by their plight, a group of philanthropists organised 'Subscribers for the relief of the distressed Blacks' to help them. From this, the 'Committee for the Relief of the Black Poor' was formed, launching a scheme to relocate many of them to a settlement in Sierra Leone. In the meantime, hundreds of Black and Asian people assembled every Saturday at two locations, one the Yorkshire Stingo at Lisson Green (and the other the White Raven in Mile End) to receive their relief of six pennies per day.

[1] *National Gazetteer of Great Britain and Ireland* (1868)

[2] Bridget Cherry and Nikolaus Pevsner, *Buildings of England: London 3* (1991), 654

[3] The discovery of the cause of cholera was made in 1854 by Dr. Snow in Soho.

[4] Nearly 40% of deaths in London between 1700 and 1750, and about a third thereafter, were of children under two years old. In 1662 the demographer John Graunt had estimated that in London of every hundred live children born, thirty-six died in their first six years and twenty-four in their first ten years. At the end of the 18th century Dr Michael Underwood, a writer on the diseases of children, wrote on the mortality rate of London children under five years during the 1790s: *'The average of births annually, within the bills of mortality, for ten successive years, as taken a few years ago (c. 1790), was 16,238; out of which were buried under five years of age 10,145, and from amongst these 7,987 were under two years. So that almost two thirds of the children born in London and its environs, become lost to society, and more than three fourths of these die under two years of age. This proves how hazardous a period that of infancy is, in this country; and I am sorry there is so much reason to be persuaded that the want of air, exercise, and a proper diet, has added unnecessarily to its dangers.'*

[5] Dorothy Wise ed. *Diary of William Tayler, Footman, 1837* (new edn. 1998).

[6] Now Ranston Street

[7] Viel Richardson, 'Labour Pains', *Marylebone Journal* (February/March 2006)

[8] F.H.W. Sheppard, *Local Government in St Marylebone 1688-1835* (1953), 168

[9] This section on the workhouse is based on Alan R Neate, *St Marylebone Workhouse* (rev. edn 2003).

Immigrants and Refugees

London, long a commercial centre and great trading port with a need of many exotic skills and materials, attracted foreign immigrants for many reasons: work in their particular trade, hope of safe harbour, economic betterment, adventure and excitement. This chapter is devoted principally to groups who came for particular reasons.

FRENCH ÉMIGRÉS

Martial Bourdin[3], a Frenchman and an anarchist, blew himself up in the grounds of Greenwich Observatory on 15 February 1894. It is not known why he chose the Observatory as a target or if indeed it was one. On investigation it was found that he attended meetings of anarchists at the Autonomie Club in Windmill Street. Bourdin lived at No.18 Great Titchfield Street and in Fitzroy Street. His funeral cortège found its way blocked by an angry crowd, which then also stoned the premises of the club.

The incident at Greenwich was immortalised by the Polish writer, Joseph Conrad in his book *The Secret Agent.*

A wave of Huguenot refugees left France for England in 1572 in the wake of the Massacre of St Bartholomew. Huguenot skills and craftsmanship were to be of enormous value to London, especially then in the Spitalfields and Clerkenwell areas. More Huguenots arrived after the revocation of the Edict of Nantes in 1685, a law which had protected their religious status in France. Some 40 to 50,000 Huguenot refugees arrived in England and because of their trades, mainly settled in London.

Claude Champion de Crespigny who arrived *c.* 1687, had social connections in London. His son became a member of the committee of the French Church in Marylebone.

The Chalon family were Huguenots who had left France for Switzerland in the 1680s only

106. *Sir Samuel Romilly.*

arriving in England in 1789. Three sons all became members of the Royal Academy – Alfred Edward, Henry Bernard and John James lived at a number of addresses including Great Titchfield Street, sometimes together. The two younger ones, John James and Alfred Edward, lived at 10 Wimpole Street (at different times). John James (1778-1854), the better known of the three, enrolled in the Royal Academy schools, exhibited there in 1801 and was also a prominent member of the Society of Painters in Watercolours. He was made an RA in 1841.

Sir Samuel Romilly (1757-1818), reformer of the judicial and penal systems, was born in Frith Street, Soho. At one time the family lived in the French Gardens which were an extension of Marylebone Gardens and part of a close-knit Huguenot community which had its own church. Later they moved to Marylebone High Street. Trained as a barrister, he travelled in Europe meeting many of the most innovative thinkers of his time. At first enthusiastic for the French Revolution he became disenchanted at the violence it provoked. He campaigned to reform the criminal law in England, especially to reduce the number of offences that merited a death sentence. He was also prominent in the campaigns to emancipate Catholics and to abolish slavery. He committed suicide in 1818, inconsolable on the death of his wife.

Fleeing the French Revolution many aristocratic families (and sometimes their servants) came to London. Some stayed for a decade or more until circumstances allowed their return to France, while others settled permanently.

The Comte d'Artois (1757-1836), the future King Charles X of France (reigned 1824-1830) lived mainly in Edinburgh but also at No. 46 Baker Street. His presence attracted others of his ilk. Some of the aristocrats, accustomed to a different life and bereft of their customary comforts made an unfavourable impression by complaining about their new surroundings. Many, having left France quickly, were impoverished, had no servants and unable to cope with the rigours of their new circumstances. It would be interesting to know if they mixed with the established, usually self-sufficient, Huguenot community and if the two sets of refugees got on.

The Comte de Montlosier arrived in London in 1794, lodging first at the west end of Marylebone Road. He was a journalist and political pamphleteer whose views elicited criticism from royalist émigrés.

Another was Jean-Gabriel Peltier a political polemicist, who also made money as a showman. He had a small guillotine built and charged admission to people who watched this device remove the heads of animals. Those at the front paid five shillings; those at the back one shilling.

There were enough Catholics amongst the new émigrés to enable them to build a place of worship of their own, called the Chapel of the Annunciation, sometimes known as the French Chapel Royal on account of attendance by members of French royalty when in London. Consecrated in 1799, it replaced a cellar at the junction of Paddington Street and Dorset Mews which had been the first place of worship used by French refugees.

JEWISH IMMIGRATION

Jews had been expelled from England in 1290 and it was not until 1656 that Oliver Cromwell permitted their return. The first arrivals were Sephardim, of Mediterranean and Middle Eastern origin. Both Charles II and James II extended protection to them.

The Ashkenazim, Jews of central and Eastern European origin also came. The Sephardim tended to be more prosperous and were merchants, dealers in jewellery or precious stones and a few specialists in medicine. The Ashkenazim tended, on arrival at least, to be poorer, unskilled and without capital, street trading, selling old clothes and keeping small shops, though there were among them notable exceptions.

After the 17th century, there were three significant periods of Jewish immigration to London, 1720 to 1730, 1890 to 1914 and 1933 onward. Each arose from cataclysmic events in Europe, accompanied by religious persecution, requiring them to seek a new home.

In the 1830s and 1840s, Bloomsbury became the Jewish residential district for the affluent classes. In the 1851 census, there were 13 Jewish householders in and around Gower Street, including Mocattas, Lewis Levy (a broker who also owned the lease to the Oxford Street Turnpike Trust), Walter Josephs and James Lewis. In 1872, the *Jewish Chronicle* noted how many Jews lived on the Bedford and Grafton estates and, in Marylebone, on the Portman estate. The very rich, the Rothschilds and the Goldsmids, were in Mayfair.

The banker, Sir Max Julius Bonn (1849-1921) of Bonn & Co., lived in Bryanston Court; Sir Felix Semon (1849-1921) a laryngologist, was in Wimpole Street; Claude Goldsmid Montefiore (1858-1938) was in Portman Square. He was a great nephew of Sir Moses Montefiore; educated at Balliol he devoted his life to philanthropy.

Julius Wolfson, 2nd Baronet of St. Marylebone (b. 1927), was head of Great Universal Stores. His father established the Wolfson Foundation in 1955, a philanthropic organisation which gives substantial donations to charities.

106a. The West London Synagogue in Upper Berkeley Street in 1872.

Sir George Lewis, England's leading society solicitor, whose clients included the Prince of Wales and Lily Langtry moved into 88 Portland Place in 1876 where his wife Elizabeth created a well attended salon in which artists and writers abounded.[1]

In Fitzrovia there were many Jewish firms specialising in clothing manufacturing, especially around Great Portland Street.

Typically, a specialist tailor might collect his work and complete it in the front room of a crowded family flat in Fitzrovia or Soho.

As mentioned on p .99 Salmon & Gluckstein established a chain of tobacconists, two of them in Oxford Street. Another Jewish tobacconist lovingly recalled in Gerry Black's book *Living up West* was at 29 Rathbone Place, where the owner supplied the famous Eiffel Tower restaurant in

Percy Street withi cigars and cigarettes. Other customers included Augustus John, Constant Lambert and Nancy Cunard.

In New Cavendish Street there was a Yiddish theatre *c.* 1935. A stage was set up in a very lage room, wich was probably a workshop during the day.

AN ASIAN IN MARYLEBONE

As we have seen on p. 36 an early Asian restaurant began in George Street in 1810. Its proprietor, Sake Dean Mahomet (1759-1851) had had a varied career before he settled in St Marylebone in 1807. He had served in the Bengal Army when very young and moved to Ireland with his patron and there married Jane Daly in 1786. It was here in 1794 that he published his autobiography.

In Marylebone Mahomed first worked in the large home of the Hon. Basil Cochrane in Portman Square who had himself recently returned from India. Cochrane established a business which gave purportedly Indian steam baths, with Mahomed as an assistant, but Mahomed developed a different skill, that of shampooing, in this sense a full-body therapeutic massage. His new bath-house sensation became popular and much copied. Mahomed went on to launch in 1809 his Hindostanee Coffee House which catered for people who liked Indian food.[2]

BLACK PERSONALITIES

The *Gentleman's Magazine* in 1764 estimated the number of 'Negro servants' in greater London at around 20,000, which was almost certainly an over-estimate. There were also concentrations of black workers in the ports of Bristol and Liverpool that dealt with goods from slave plantations.

Generally we know only of black people of the 18th century in detail if, by chance, they had received some education and had managed to prosper because of it, such as the young girl, Dido Belle, who became the amanuensis to Lord Mansfield, the Lord Chief Justice, at his home, Kenwood House in Highgate. He left her sufficient money on his death to buy a house near Hanover Square.

The black men that are mostly cited in this period are Ignatius Sancho, Quobna Cugoano and Olaudah Equiano. The first two had no connection with Marylebone, except that Cugoano was well known to the Cosways and indeed featured in one of the artist's paintings. We do know more about Equiano. He was born *c.* 1745 in what is now Nigeria, was kidnapped at the age of ten and taken to the West Indies and then on to Virginia where he was sold to a planter called Campbell, probably the same Alexander Campbell who later, during the long debates in Parliament on the abolition of slavery, spoke against abolition. Equiano was then passed on to a new master, Michael Pascal, a naval man, who renamed him Gustavus Vassa and brought him to England in 1754. He was baptised as a Christian in St Margaret's Westminster in 1759 and stated to be 12 years of age. Oddly enough, this was the same church in which Ignatius Sancho had been married two months earlier. He spent at least twelve years on ships and gradually took an interest in the abolition of slavery and welfare of other black people. In 1786 he became involved with resettling blacks in Sierra Leone and in the abolition movement. He returned to London in 1787, lived in Holborn and the following year moved on to 13 Tottenham Street in Fitzrovia. In 1789 he was in Riding House Street near the Middlesex Hospital. It was here that he published his *Narrative* of his travels and experiences, with 300 subscribers who included artists, abolitionists, aristocrats, the Prince of Wales, Cosway, Wedgwood and Cugoano. A year later he moved to Covent Garden.[3]

[1]   Gerry Black, *Living up West* (1994), 28

[2]   Michael H Fisher, 'Asians in Westminster during the Early Nineteenth Century', *Westminster History Review* 5 (2007)

[3]   Vincent Carretta, 'Friends of Freedom: Three African-British Men of Letters in Eighteenth-Century Westminster', *Westminster History Review* 3 (1999)

Falling Foul

AT THE OLD BAILEY

The early trial records of the Old Bailey reveal many cases in Marylebone involving larceny, murder, attempted murder, infanticide, bigamy, burglary, kidnapping and street crimes including highway robbery. The area around the Oxford Market produced substantial numbers of offenders who were convicted of larceny, pickpocketing and burglary.

Sentences were, by 20th-century standards, severe, and clemency by reason of one's disadvantaged circumstances unknown though youth was sometimes taken into account. In the period 1820-1, James Jordan (age 13), William Donald (12) and Thomas Steers (13) were sentenced to death for stealing six silver spoons from a house in William Street, Manchester Square although they were 'recommended to mercy on account of their youth.' William Arnold (20) was sentenced to death for assaulting Thomas Allison 'on the King's highway, at St. Marylebone' and 'putting him in fear, and taking from his person, and against his will, one pound bank note.' George Palmer (15) was sentenced to death for assaulting and stealing from John Sanderson on Marylebone High Street. George Edwards (27) offered no defence and was sentenced to death for assaulting Henry Berridge on the Edgware Road and stealing his watch.

THE CATO STREET CONSPIRACY

Cato Street, east of Edgware Road and just off Harrowby Street, was the centre of a famous political conspiracy.

In the years after the Napoleonic Wars from 1815 England experienced social, economic and political upheavals. The distress and discontent were manifested in a series of disturbances. A group of radicals called the Society of Spencean Philanthropists, after the radical Thomas Spence (1750-1814), pledged to fulfil his advocacy of reform brought about by a violent revolution and, as part of this, the ideal of common ownership of land. One of the conspirators William Davidson, born in Jamaica in 1781, was radicalised by the events after 1815 and particularly by the 1819 'Peterloo Massacre' in Manchester where a cavalry charge to break up a reformist meeting had killed eleven people and injured many more. Davidson joined the Marylebone Union Reading Society where he met another soon-to-be conspirator, John Harrison. Shortly after, Davidson joined the Spenceans in whose company he met Arthur Thistlewood.

In 1817, John Stafford, Chief Clerk at Bow Street, who recruited Home Office spies, asked a police officer, George Ruthven, to join the Spenceans under cover. Ruthven in 1820 discovered that the group planned an armed uprising. The conspirators had believed that the entire cabinet was to dine with Lord Harrowby on 23 February, at No. 44 Grosvenor Square. Their plan was to assassinate the cabinet members and inspire a widespread armed uprising. Once killed, the heads of Sidmouth (the Home Secretary) and his supporter Lord Castlereagh would be carried away for display on pikes on Westminster Bridge. As a base, the group rented a small, two-storey building in Cato Street, comprising a ground floor and a hayloft.

107. The premises in Cato Street used by the conspirators.

108. *The arrest of the Cato Street conspirators in 1820. From a drawing by George Cruikshank.*

One of the group's supporters, Thomas Edwards, probably a government spy, told Stafford of the plan. The authorities responded by dispatching men from the Second Battalion of the Coldstream Guards as well as police officers from Bow Street. Ruthven was sent to the Horse and Groom which overlooked the premises in Cato Street and at seven thirty that evening twelve police officers joined him, but the Coldstream Guards had not yet arrived. Nevertheless, Ruthven led his men to the hayloft. A skirmish followed during which Thistlewood killed one of the officers with a sword. Although Thistlewood, Harrison and two others escaped, they were soon arrested.

Eleven men were charged as conspirators and on 28 April, Thistlewood, Davidson and three others, Ings, Brunt and Tidd, were found guilty of high treason and sentenced to death by execution at Newgate. They were spared being drawn and quartered because of public sympathy.

The Traveller, May 1820 recorded that:

'The executioner, who trembled much, was a long time tying up the prisoners; while this operation was going on a dead silence prevailed among the crowd, but the moment the drop fell, the general feeling was manifested by deep sighs and groans. Ings and Brunt were those only who manifested pain while hanging. The former writhed for some moments; but the latter for several minutes seemed, from the horrifying contortions of his countenance, to be suffering the most excruciating torture.'

After death, the head of each of the hanged men was severed. The executioner displayed each head to the crowd proclaiming, 'This is the head of a traitor.' The other conspirators were transported for life.

After the event the name of the street was changed to Horace Street but later reverted and there is now a blue plaque marking the event at what is now No. 1A Cato Street.

THE DRUCE CASE AND THE PORTLANDS

A shop in Baker Street became in 1896 the focus of a most extraordinary case when Anna Maria Druce laid claim to the inheritance of the 5th Duke of Portland (1800-79) on behalf of her son. She claimed that her father-in-law, Thomas Charles Druce (died 1864), had been in fact the obsessively reclusive 5th Duke who as part of his alter ego, owned the Baker Street Bazaar. Tired of his disguise and wanting to return to his eccentric insularity, Portland, she claimed, had faked the death of Druce and his burial in Highgate Cemetery.

Mrs Druce applied to have the coffin of her father-in-law opened to see whether it contained his body, but it was not until 1907 that this was allowed – to reveal the remains of Thomas Druce. Mrs Druce had, surprisingly, many supporters in her campaign and even a company was established to capitalise on the inheritance. In the aftermath of the denouement, two witnesses were charged with perjury, and another witness and Anna Maria were confined to asylums.

The Bazaar later traded as a furniture store and Druce estate agents from 37, 39, 55 and 57 Baker Street. Estate agents of that name still operate in Weymouth Street.

THE BLACKOUT RIPPER

During the Blitz in 1942 Londoners took refuge in underground train stations, cellars and air raid shelters. In blackout conditions, amidst strangers whom one was obliged to trust, women were particularly vulnerable. In one week, Gordon Frederick Cummins, whom the newspapers termed the *Blackout Ripper*, murdered four women, attacking two others.

On the morning of Sunday 9 February the body of teacher Evelyn Hamilton was found in an air raid shelter in Montagu Place. She had been strangled and her handbag was stolen. She was the first of the four victims to be murdered. Cummins, a 28-year-old RAF cadet, was arrested on 16 February in St. John's Wood – he had abandoned his marked gas mask at the scene of his last murder. He was tried in April 1942 and executed at Wandsworth Prison on 25 June.

THE BAKER STREET BANK ROBBERY

Those responsible for the theft of a large amount of money, jewellery and (possibly) 'incriminating information' from safety deposit boxes in Lloyd's Bank, Baker Street in September 1971 were never caught. Mystery surrounded the raid and the subsequent investigation especially when at the height of press coverage the government issued a D Notice, a so-called gagging-order, to prevent further disclosures.

After the story disappeared from the press, rumours continued, but the raid is due to be aired again in 2008 with the release of a new film, called *The Bank Job*, written by Dick Clement and Ian La Frenais, which claims to be based on information from someone who knew a great deal about the raid. The news of this led *The Independent* in September 2007 to repeat a claim that the raid was staged by MI5 to recover compromising pictures of Princess Margaret on the Caribbean island of Mustique. Other commentators have hinted at a cover-up involving high-ranking police officers, the intelligence service and influential people .

THE BALCOMBE STREET SIEGE

Unremarkable Balcombe Street, running to the east of Marylebone Station, became in December 1975 the focus of newspaper headlines, when four IRA terrorists holed up at No. 22b, taking the occupants, Sheila Matthews and her husband John hostage.

The men, Hugh Doherty, Martin O'Connell, Eddie Butler and Harry Duggan, were being pursued by police after an attack on a restaurant in Mayfair. This occurred after the collapse of the IRA's ceasefire of 1974-5, and the murder of Ross McWhirter, co-editor of the *Guiness Book of Records* in retaliation for his offer of a reward for information leading to their arrest.

The gang demanded safe passage to Ireland, but the police refused a deal. On 12 December, after six days of siege, the men surrendered. The hostages were released and millions watched this on television. The four men were sentenced to life, but were released in 1999 under the terms of the Good Friday Agreement.

Some Entertainments

EARLY PLACES

J. T. Smith, in his *Book for a Rainy Day* (1772), described a walk through Marylebone.

'I well remember that, after we had passed Portland Chapel[1], there were fields all the way on either side. The highway was irregular ... and that when we had crossed the New Road, there was a turnstile at the entrance of a meadow, leading to a little old public-house ... the *Queen's Head and Artichoke*[2]...'A little beyond a nest of small houses opening also into fields, over which we walked to the *Jew's Harp House* Tavern and Tea-Gardens. On the eastern side of the house there was a trap-ball-ground; the western side served for a tennis-hall; there were also public and private skittle-grounds.'

Spectator sports and leisure activities abounded in Marylebone from an early period. Earliest of course was the hunting in what was Marylebone Fields *(see p. 42)* from the 16th century. From the 17th century Marylebone Gardens *(p. 53)* featured bowling and then developed into a pleasure garden. Other entertainments included violent sports – bare-knuckle fighting and cock- and dog-fighting, which attracted even wider audiences than the more genteel pleasures staged by Marylebone Gardens.

JAMES FIGG – CHAMPION FIGHTER

For 11 years between 1719 and 1730, James Figg (1695-1734) was the first bare-knuckle fighting champion of England. In addition, he was an accomplished wrestler, fencer and fighter with cudgels or quarterstaffs. Originally with backing from a patron, the Earl of Peterborough, he opened a fighting academy on a site at the Tottenham Court Road end of Oxford Street. Later he and James Broughton, another pugilist, opened an amphitheatre known as the Boarded

109. *James Figg. left, spars with his pupil, James Broughton, who succeeded him as bare-knuckle champion.*

House near Adam and Eve Court just off Oxford Street, between Berners and Winsley Streets. Visiting challengers came to test their skills at organised fights in the 1720s. The bouts included women fighters and advertising featured such allurements as 'Mrs Stokes-City Championess, versus the Hibernian-heroine' to attract audiences. Animal fights also featured.

Figg also operated an academy, advertising himself as: 'James Figg Master of ye Noble Science of Defence on y right hand of Oxford Road near Adam and Eve Court. Teaches y use of y small backsword and Quarterstaff at home and abroad.' Of imposing stature at six feet, Figg lost only once in over 270 fights.

Figg bested Edward ('Ned') Sutton at a match in front of an audience which included Sir Robert Walpole, then the Prime Minister. The fight involved bare-knuckles, sword and cudgels. A poem by James Byrom described the bout:

Long was the great Figg, by the prize-fighting
   swains
Sole monarch acknowledged of Marybone plains
To the towns, far and near, did his valour extend,'
   After a bloody contest Figg won:
Tho' Sutton, disabled as soon as he hit him,
Would still have fought on, but Jove would
   not permit him;
'Twas his fate, not his fault, that constrain'd
   him to yield,
And thus the great Figg became lord of the
   field.

Hogarth painted Figg's portrait and newspapers of the day reported his death in 1734 at the age of forty. He was a friend of the notorious thief and prison escaper, Jack Sheppard, who stopped at Figg's establishment in Oxford Street in 1724 on his way from Newgate to execution at Tyburn. In 1992, Figg was inducted into the International Boxing Hall of Fame.

SOME NOTABLE THEATRES

The Queen's Bazaar was on the north side at what is now 152 Oxford Street. It was originally built to show dioramas *(see p. 126)* – a form of panoramic view – by the artists Clarkson Stanfield and David Roberts. It was later described as a Ladies' Bazaar for the Sale of Miscellaneous Articles and galleries for the reception and display of works of art. In 1836 it opened as a theatre named after the (then) Princess Victoria as the **Princess Theatre**. After

operating unsuccessfully with promenade concerts, the buildings were altered (with decor by Crace & Son) and it reopened in September 1840. The premises stretched to Eastcastle Street on the north. Productions included an opera 1842 by Vincenzo Bellini entitled *La Sonnambula*. Later, the Irish actor and playwright, Dionysius Lardner Boursiquot, known for melodramas, chose the Princess Theatre to stage nine plays: *The Corsican Brothers* (1852), *La Dame de Pique; or, The Vampire* (1852), *The Prima Donna* (1852), *After Dark, A Tale of London* (1868), *Presumptive Evidence* (1869), and *Paul Lafarge, A Dark Night's Work*, and *The Raparee* (1870). In addition, revivals of Shakespeare also ran. Ellen Terry made her stage debut here in 1856 at the age of eight.

THE ROYAL SUSSEX AND ROYAL MARYLEBONE THEATRES

Before the establishment of a purpose-built theatre in Marylebone, there were companies of

110. The Princess Theatre in Oxford Street.

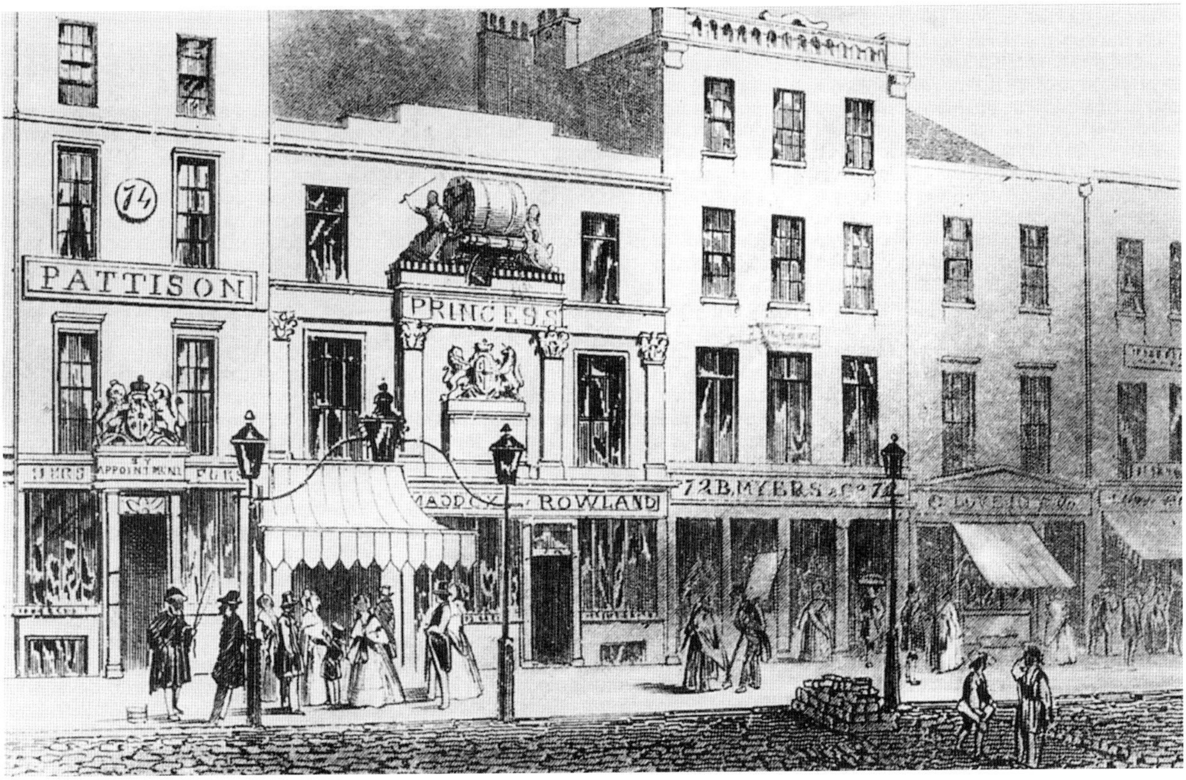

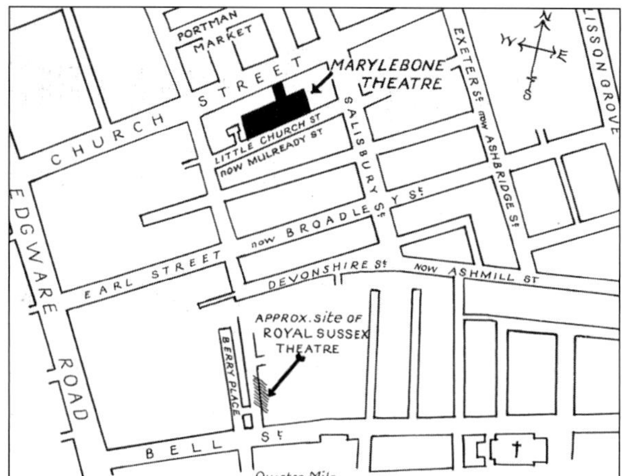

111. *Map showing the position of the two old theatres in Lisson Green. (From* The Old Marylebone Theatre, *published by the St Marylebone Society, 1960)*

strolling players. In 1801 one of these, the New Travelling Theatre, performed an opera and a pantomime in Lisson Green. The earliest theatre opened in October 1831 called the Royal Sussex Subscription Theatre, located on the north side of Bell Street in Lisson Green. According to Malcolm Morley,

> The theatre was constructed of wood, the interior having a decorative lining of paper. Poles were placed in the ground to strengthen the walls whilst the timbers generally were covered with canvas … The Royal Sussex (as the theatre was then called) had accommodation for seven hundred people.

However, the Royal Sussex was not licensed to charge for performances and could only get money for refreshments, and with competition in 1832 from a new theatre nearby, the Royal Pavilion West, the owner of the Sussex went bankrupt and finished in Whitecross debtors' prison. The Royal Pavilion, also unlicensed to charge for tickets, resorted to giving them with overpriced bakery products in a nearby shop.

The opening of the Royal Pavilion began a hundred years of theatre on its site, spanning a bewildering number of name changes and rebuilding. The theatre took over two stable yards at the back of houses in Church Street, the entrance being in what is now Mulready Street).

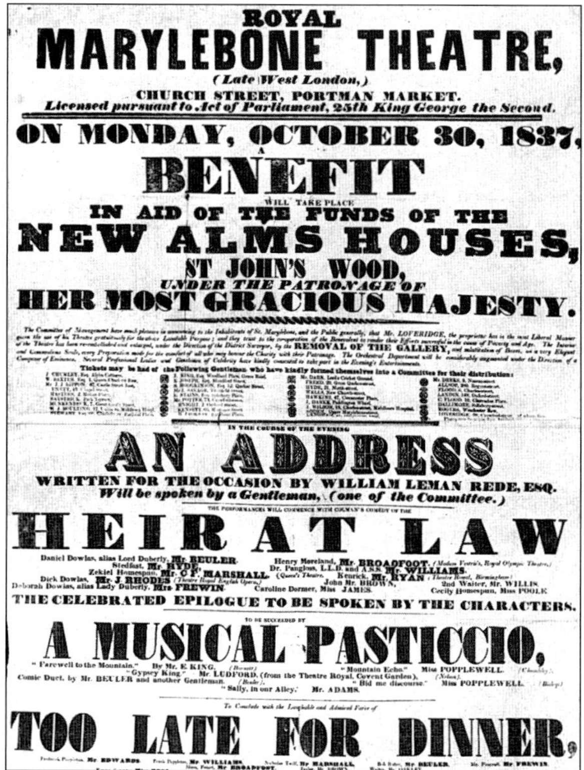

112. *An early playbill of the Royal Marylebone Theatre.*

opening with a revival of a popular gothic melodrama *The Old Oak Chestnut*.

As recounted by Malcolm Morley, the Royal Pavilion staged the first 'dog drama'. These were plays where dogs, specifically trained to perform as characters, were the protagonists, attacking evil-doers and rescuing or succouring victims. Dog Drama continued in playhouses on the fringes of London for another thirty years.

An indication of the calibre of audiences attending may be inferred from a notice to the 'Frequenters of this Theatre … that the Gallery Audience [has occasionally] interrupted the business', adding that measures would be taken to 'shut up the Gallery altogether.' The disruptive audience was a recurring complaint.

The theatre was renamed the Portman Theatre in 1835 and then refurbished and reopened as the Royal Marylebone Theatre in 1837. The productions were a mix of spectacle, farce, melodrama and tragedy. Pessimistically, the

113. John Loveridge, owner of the Royal.

weekly *Figaro in London* noted, 'We fear its locality, and its smallness will always preclude its being profitable.'

Eventually, the lease of the freehold in Church Street was purchased by John Loveridge, a self-made local businessman who, having prospered in a shop in Crawford Street to the south of Marylebone Road, had begun to buy or lease property in the vicinity. He determined to have the entrance of the theatre in Church Street. As he was not himself a theatre man, he leased the premises periodically to tenants who were: he then shared the receipts with the tenant in a specified proportion. Loveridge, local and respected, managed to secure the first licence for the theatre. Another renaming and rebuilding of the Royal Marylebone, this time to accommodate 2000 people, took place in 1847 when it emerged as the Theatre Royal, Marylebone. During this incarnation, it experienced prosperity performing melodrama, the most popular event being the Christmas pantomime. In 1850, when a serious monologue was performed before the main attraction, the audience objected demanding the pantomime. Under the management of Joseph Cave in 1858 'fantastic illusions' were produced with one of the earliest uses of electricity in the theatre. The Theatre Royal's stage was celebrated for its depth possibly having the largest in London.

By 1866, the theatre had become the Royal Alfred after the second son of Queen Victoria, and later was renamed the Royal Marylebone and then the Royal West London. In 1904, the young Charlie Chaplin performed the role of Billy in *Sherlock Holmes*. Two years later, exhibitions of moving pictures gradually replaced drama and this was confirmed in 1913 when the New Biograph Trading Company took over, renaming the building the West London Cinema and also staged wrestling and boxing.

Errol Sherson in his work *London's Lost Theatres of the Nineteenth Century* (1925) wrote that the theatre was not successful because 'the immediate neighbourhood ... and the regular frequenters of the theatre preferred stronger fare than ... other earnest members of that profession could provide, adding that 'Playgoers would not go to Church Street, Edgware Road with all its unpleasant surroundings [and] it gradually fell to the rank of a third-rate house for cheap entertainment.' The building was damaged in the Second World War and by 1960 was derelict.[3]

Tucked away in Gateforth Street is a relatively new theatre, The Cockpit, designed by Ed Mendelssohn, opened *c*.1964 and was principally used by theatre groups attached to educational establishments or was booked by touring groups, or for experimental plays. Its most satisfying period was that under the three-year aegis of Abigail Morris in the 1990s when it was used by the Soho Theatre.

SARAH SIDDONS

Sarah Siddons (1755-1831) the 'undisputed queen of Drury Lane' lived at 27 Upper Baker Street (since March 1930 part of Baker Street) from 1817 until 1831. The daughter of an actor-manager Roger Kemble and sister of Charles Kemble, also a famous actor, she started her

114. Sarah Siddons.

career in provincial theatre, opening in the role of Portia in the *Merchant of Venice* in 1775 at the Theatre Royal, Drury Lane. She was not a success in that very large venue and her contract was not renewed. However she returned after 6 years and was a sensational success in David Garrick's production of a play by Thomas Southerne entitled *Isabella*. She socialised among the literati and the aristocracy of London numbering the indefatigable Samuel Johnson and Edmund Burke among her acquaintances. She was reputed to earn £1,000 for eighty nights (about £12 per night), a vast sum then. In her will, she left her leasehold house in Upper Baker Street to her daughter Cecilia, together with her 'carriages, horses, plate, pictures, books, wine, and furniture, and all the money in the house and at the banker's.' Her house, now demolished, was according to conflicting authorities, on the site of the Lost Property Office at No. 200 Baker Street, or else at No. 226. She is buried in St Mary's Cemetery at Paddington Green, just to the west of the Edgware Road.

115. Sarah Siddons' house in Upper Baker Street.

THE DIORAMA

The kaleidoscope of entertainments during the 18th and, particularly, the 19th centuries grew with technical developments. Exhibitions, extravaganzas and sensational shows were staged to attract, inform and titillate. Panoramas showing views of famous sites, foreign landscapes and contemporary events were popular. Louis Daguerre (1787-1851), inventor of one of the earliest photographic processes,

116. The Diorama in Regent's Park.

known as 'daguerreotypes' also produced the Diorama. The first one, opened in Paris in 1822, gave an exciting three-dimensional effect to images, with an illusion of movement, most popular being catastrophes and battles.

A Diorama opened in 1823 on the south-east corner of Regent's Park at 18 Park Square East. It was designed by A. C. Pugin and the engineer James Morgan under the direction of Daguerre's brother-in-law, James Arrowsmith.

The auditorium, which could take up to 200 people, was rotated mechanically 73° so the audience could view either of two stages. *Trompe l'oeil* scenes were painted on calico cloths 72' high and 40' wide with special effects comprising music and lighting. The show lasted about thirty minutes, although viewers could stay and see the sequence repeated. In 1830, *The Times* noted:

'The views at the Diorama are again changed, and France and Switzerland are once more placed before our eyes without our encountering the nausea of crossing the Channel, the roguery of continental innkeepers, and all the other innumerable and indescribable miseries of foreign travel.'

The Diorama, however, was not a great commercial success, closing in 1851, and it became a Baptist chapel at the expense of Sir Samuel Morton Peto, and later became the Arthur Stanley Institute of Rheumatic Diseases; it was renovated in the 1990s for use as an Arts Centre.

THE COLOSSEUM

When the dome of St Paul's was covered in scaffolding for repairs in 1821, Thomas Hornor, a surveyor, erected a vertiginous vantage point above the ball and cross, and was able to make over 2,000 sketches of the views across London. Hornor secured financial backing to house a vast panorama based on his drawings in a building in the Outer Circle, just north of the Diorama. The domed Colosseum, designed by Decimus Burton, opened in 1829.

It was a sixteen-sided building, about 130 feet in diameter, with a Doric portico and cupola. It was visited by more than one million people in

117. *The Colosseum in Regent's Park.*

the first fifteen years, and also housed a sculpture saloon, a landscaped garden and a 300-foot conservatory filled with exotic plants. The circular verandah on the roof housed a camera obscura. In 1834, an arena was installed for the new sport of roller-skating. On 21 February 1846 *The Illustrated London News* advertised the Colosseum and all its delights declaring, 'Patronized and Visited by Her Most Gracious Majesty and His Royal Highness Prince Albert–Six Exhibitions in One, comprising–Panorama of London by Day–The Museum of Sculpture Arabesque Conservatories–Gorgeous Gothic Aviary–Classic Ruins–Swiss Cottage and Mont Blanc, with Mountain Torrent. A Grand Orchestral Organ, on which the most admired Overtures are played.' A Cyclorama was added which gave a realistic representation of the earthquake of Lisbon and, according to the journalist Edmund Yates, the effect was 'most terrifying ... frightful rumblings from under your feet increased the horror ... Never was better value in fright given for money.'

Initially a commercial success, the Colosseum was demolished in 1875 and replaced by the High Victorian mansion flats faced with Bath Stone (instead of the Nash stucco) comprising Cambridge Gate between 1876 and 1880. The architects were Archer & Green.

THE BAKER STREET BAZAAR

The Baker Street Bazaar was first established for the sale of horses. In 1829 it advertised a 'magnificent exhibition of musical and mechanical automata, comprising nearly twenty different subjects, including the celebrated musical lady, juvenile artist, magician, ropedancer, and walking figure; also a magnificent classic vase, made by order of Napoleon; together with a serpent, birds, insects, and other subjects of natural history; the whole displaying, by their exact imitations of animated nature, the wonderful powers of mechanism.' It was once owned by Thomas Charles Druce (*see p 121*).

In 1834, the Bazaar announced its forthcoming Padorama – a mechanical-pictorial exhibition.

The early railways had created great interest in travel in Britain and the Bazaar exhibit comprised 10,000 square feet of dioramic strip wound on drums showing the most scenic parts of the country traversed by the Liverpool & Manchester Railway. It also used model railway stock complete with model passengers and cattle. An advertisement in *The Times* recorded that it was an 'exact replica' of the route and encouraged 'everyone of our juvenile friends ... to see it, as it is very instructive for youth.' The Padorama, though ingenious, was short lived.

The Bazaar also had a 'grand moving diorama of Hindustan from Fort William, Bengal to Gangoutri in the Himalayas.' In 1842 the Bazaar advertised the earliest artificial ice-rink in the country, a 'Glaciarium – a Frozen Lake' where people could skate without fear of falling through ice. However, the ice was made of chemicals including hogs lard and melted sulphur and the combination of the nauseous smell and the smallness of the rink meant commercial failure.

MADAME TUSSAUD AND THE BAKER STREET BAZAAR

Born Marie Grosholz in 1761 in Strasbourg, Mme Tussaud lived a long and adventurous life, dying in 1850. From her mother's employer, a doctor Philippe Curtius, who in 1770 opened an exhibition of life-size wax figures at the Palais Royale in Paris, Marie learned the techniques of wax modelling.

In Paris, in 1777, she may have modelled the head of Voltaire and by 1780, she had become an art tutor to Louis XVI's sister. At the outbreak of the Revolution, she returned from Versailles to Paris putting her skills to use to model the heads of some of the victims of *Le Terroir* and its assistant the newly invented guillotine. She married Francois Tussaud in 1795, but in 1802 left France, showing her collection around Britain. She toured it by caravan until in 1835 she settled it at the Baker Street Bazaar. In a separate room she displayed the cautionary relics of the French Revolution, a room which *Punch* dubbed in 1846 the 'Chamber of Horrors'. Some 34 years after her death, the collection remained a popular tourist

attraction and her grandson directed the move to new premises in Marylebone Road in 1884. It continues to allure tourists.

An 1842 guidebook stated that 'Visitors entering the Bazaar from Baker Street proceed to a saloon richly decorated with mirrored embellishments. Here sits an aged lady, with an accent which proclaims her Gallic origins. Were she motionless, you would take her for a piece of waxwork. This is Madame Tussaud, a lady who is in herself an Exhibition.'

The Royal Smithfield Club held its annual Cattle Show at the Bazaar from 1839 to 1861. Prince Albert was an exhibitor here, carrying off several prizes in 1844 and 1850.

118. Madame Tussaud and below (119), the exhibition building in Marylebone Road c. 1905.

BERTOLOTTO AND HIS FLEA CIRCUS

An unusual but popular fairground attraction in the 19th century were flea circuses which were first advertised in England in the 1830s. One of the most famous was that of Louis Bertolotto, whose 'Extraordinary Exhibition of the Industrious Fleas' performed in London, New York and Canada. Bertolotto had a flea workshop in Marylebone which was recorded by Francis Buckland in *Curiosities of Natural History* when he paid a visit there:

> 'In the month of July 1856, I discovered an individual who for twenty years had devoted his life to the intellectual training of fleas. He carried on his operations in a little room in Marylebone Street, London. I entered, and saw fleas here, fleas there, fleas everywhere; no less than sixty fleas imprisoned and sentenced to hard labour for life. All of them were luckily chained, or fastened in some way or other, so that escape and subsequent feasting upon visitors was impossible.'

Buckland went on to describe how the fleas were trained to perform, where Bertolotto got his fleas from and also commented on a less obvious problem with transit:

> 'When our friend in Marylebone makes his annual tour into the provinces, his wife sends him weekly a supply of fleas in the corner of an envelope, packed in tissue-paper. She is careful not to put them in the corner where the stamp goes, as the post-office clerk would, with his stamp-marker, at one blow, smash the whole of the stock.'

Bertolotto published *The History of the Flea with Notes and Observations* during the 1830s.

THE QUEEN'S HEAD AND ARTICHOKE

The Queen's Head and Artichoke dated from the 16th century and could, Ann Saunders thinks, have been originally a hunting lodge for Henry VIII's park. It was in the south-east corner of the Crown Estate, just west of today's Albany Street and about 500 yards north of the Marylebone Road. It was pleasantly rural, renowned for its hospitality and ales and had a skittle ground. It also provided tea, cakes, bowls and a 'bumble-puppy' ground – an old form of tennis. In 1772 J.T.Smith described it as 'much weather-beaten'.

120.   *The Queen's Head and Artichoke, c. 1750.*

It was demolished when Regent's Park was laid out and we next find a pub of that name in Albany Street when that road was formed. Henceforth it would be part of the parish of St Pancras rather than Marylebone.

TAVERNS IN MARYLEBONE HIGH STREET

On the west side, there are three notable public houses whose buildings date from the mid to late 19th century when the Howard de Walden Estate did much rebuilding as the 99-year leases fell in. These are the Black Horse of 1892 by W. Bratford, in an ornate Jacobean style, the Queen's Head of 1863, Italianate with bold lettering and the Old Rising Sun, 1866 Italianate.

MUSIC AND CONCERT HALLS

'Light Music' began in the late 1800s with a proliferation of light orchestras in resorts and spas and, in particular, in Paris, where the creative performance arts attracted urbanites of all classes.

The Oxford Music Hall at what is now 14-16 Oxford Street was built *c.*1859 and survived in one guise or another until 1926 when it was demolished for a Lyons restaurant.

Marylebone, uniquely, had three Concert Halls of note, of which one survives.

The Wigmore Hall (formerly the Bechstein

121. *The Bechstein Hall in Wigmore Street, then part of the showrooms of Bechstein pianos. During the First World War it became the Wigmore Hall.*

Hall) is at 36 Wigmore Street. Small and elegant, it seats 600 for concerts. It opened on 31 May 1901 partly as an advertisement for the German piano company, Bechstein, whose showrooms occupied the street frontage. The Hall was then approached by a passageway leading from the street. The building was designed by Thomas Collcutt, architect of the Savoy Hotel, in an Edwardian Renaissance style.

Over the stage is a famous cupola designed by Gerald Moira. The painting by Frank Lynn Jenkins depicts the Soul of Music. Its acoustics attracted great artists such as Artur Schnabel, Pablo Sarasate, Percy Grainger, Myra Hess, Artur Rubinstein and Camille Saint-Saëns.

During the First World War, the Hall was seized as 'enemy property' – indeed one of the two Bechstein owners was an officer in the German army. The Hall, showroom and contents were sold at auction in November 1916 to Debenham's, together with 137 pianos, for a knockdown price of £56,500. It re-opened as the Wigmore Hall on 16 January 1917 with a presentation of three Beethoven violin sonatas, though German pianos were banned and Schumann and Wagner were sung in English.

Eminent musicians and composers such as Janacek in 1926, Ethel Smyth in 1928 and Prokofiev in 1931, played at the Hall before the last war, and Ashkenazy, Schwarzkopf, Richter and Benjamin Britten in more modern times. From the 1960s it has confirmed its international reputation as a leading recital hall. Much of the credit for this must go to a self-effacing Australian, William Lyne, who was on a year's sabbatical from the Australian Broadcasting Commission when he took over in 1966 – he stayed for 37 years. In 2003 a five-hour gala with

122.   *The Queen's Hall in Langham Place, where the Proms began.*

no fewer than thirty-two soloists was performed to mark his long and creative reign at the Wigmore Hall.

The Hall was completely refurbished in 2004 and in 2005 the Wigmore Hall Trust purchased its freehold.

St. George's Hall at 4 Langham Place opened in April 1867 for the New Philharmonic Society; it accommodated 800 to 900 people. The architect was John Taylor of Whitehall. It presented both music and musical theatre for many years and was the headquarters of the London Academy of Music; it was later converted to use as a skating rink. The Hall was acquired in 1933 by Eric Maschwitz for the BBC for broadcasts of vaudeville, comedy and revue, opening as a theatre in November 1933. The hall was extensively damaged by bombing in March 1941 and the studios moved to the Aeolian Hall in New Bond Street. The building was demolished in 1966 the site, together with that of the Queen's Hall was used for the construction of the St. George's Hotel and Henry Wood House.

The Queens's Hall, on the corner with Riding House Street, was opened in 1893. A handsome building, built as a colosseum with paired corinthian columns on its upper balcony and the roundels of the heads of famous composers set both at ground level and on the balconies, it was designed by Thomas Edward Knightley.

It was here on 10 August 1895 that Henry Wood conducted the first Promenade Concert, though the idea of having a cleared arena so that many of the audience could walk about during performances had originally been tried in 1838 at what is now the Lyceum Theatre. The project was under the leadership of Robert Newman. The Proms and the Queen's Hall became an important part of London's musical life. Eventually the music publishers, Chappell's, assumed the management of the Proms until 1927 when the BBC took them under their wing until this day.

The Hall was bombed in 1940, managed to survive, but a second hit in 1941 burned it virtually to the ground.

123. Hector Berlioz.

Carl Maria Von Weber (1786-1826), expelled from Wurttemberg for refusing military service, came to London where he lived at what was then No. 91, Great Portland Street. He became a highly successful pianist, composer and conductor but died young of consumption

Close by, at No. 103, another German composer, **Felix Mendelssohn** (1809-1847) stayed on his many visits to London.

[1] In Great Portland Street, built in 1766.

[2] See p. 130.

[3] Much of the information for this section is derived from *The Old Marylebone Theatre*, published by the St Marylebone Society (1960)

COMPOSERS AND MUSICIANS

Hector Berlioz (1803-69) the French composer, lived at No. 58 Queen Anne Street between May and July 1851, when he was invited to judge musical instruments at the Great Exhibition. He did not find the task congenial, but stayed, unlike some of the other judges, to the end, albeit complaining. His compensation lay in the active musical life of London. The French exhibits were judged the best. In 1852 he lived at 10 Old Cavendish Street and in 1853 had moved to No. 17.

Local Affairs

The outlying village of Marylebone became in little more than two generations in the mid-18th century, part of the metropolis. The laws, the institutions of local government and the enfranchisement of its residents reflect this. The title of F.H.W. Sheppard's book, *Local Government in St. Marylebone 1688 to 1835*[1] (1958) belies the instructive entertainment to be had from its reading. From it emerge the personalities and talents of two key men, William Thomas (originally an employee of the 1st Earl of Oxford and then of his son, Edward Harley, from 1724) and John Jones, the Vestry Clerk of the parish of St. Marylebone (1770 to 1813). Both were important in the development of Marylebone.

BACKGROUND

In the Middle Ages most local administration was carried out by the manors via their courts, but from the late 16th century more and more responsibilities were put on the parishes, especially the relief of the poor. Parish meetings were usually in the vestry room of the local church, hence the term 'vestry' to denote an administrative unit. Any ratepayer could attend an 'open' vestry and be responsible for electing the small number of unpaid officials, such as someone to survey and maintain the highways, to pay out poor relief, to bundle beggars and other such threats out of the parish before they became a charge on the rates, to examine the quality of ale and bread, and so on. Not everyone wanted to be a parish official and paid someone else to do it for him when it was his turn.

St Marylebone was an 'open' vestry until 1768. Thereafter, until 1832, it became a 'select' vestry, that is, it was enabled by an Act of Parliament to have an elite and self-selecting group of leading residents to manage affairs without the nuisance of awkward questions from lesser mortals. During the 18th century other authorities were established with their own remits, such as the Turnpike Trusts or Paving Boards which looked after lighting and paving on private estates.

ENFRANCHISEMENT

A succession of Acts from 1832 gradually established democracy and enfranchisement as we know it today and in 1855 the Metropolitan Board of Works was formed with a limited remit to govern certain aspects of London's activities, in particular the improvement of the sewage system, by then at the point of breakdown.

In 1867, by a Representation of the People Act, the franchise was reformed so that each male over 21 who occupied as either an owner or tenant for twelve months a separate dwelling (without regard to value, or lodgings of £10 unfurnished) was enfranchised. This substantially extended the electorate and gradually, but slowly, women got the vote and were entitled to stand for office.

In 1889 the London County Council, with considerable powers over the metropolis, was established, and ten years later the various vestries and other authorities in Inner London were condensed into 27 metropolitan boroughs, whereupon the vestry of St. Marylebone became the borough of St. Marylebone.

In 1965, London's borders were extended into the surrounding counties, the LCC was abolished and in its place the Greater London Council was formed. At this time Marylebone became part of the City of Westminster, its local interests subsumed in the greater interests of central London.

THE RATES

In 1768, the parish levied four rates: for the Poor, for the maintenance of highways and for cleaning them, for the provision of rudimentary lighting in some areas, and to pay watchmen – this was before the establishment of the Metropolitan Police in 1829. These rates were collected by men who were bonded as insurance against discrepancies and defalcations. The Vestry Clerk audited their books to ensure accuracy.

WILLIAM THOMAS

William Thomas began work with the Harley family in or about 1708. When George I came to the throne in 1714, the Tories were out, the Whigs were in, and the 1st Earl of Oxford, Robert Harley, was sent to the Tower for high treason.

Thomas was, on a reliable recommendation of his honesty and assiduity, taken on as Steward of the manor of Tyburn in 1721 by the young Edward Harley, who became the 2nd Earl in 1724. Thomas then became one of the original trustees named in the local Turnpike Act of 1721 and, in 1734, its chairman. As Steward of the manor until 1746, he collected rent, oversaw the control of new buildings and the abatement of nuisances, which included dealing with publicans in breach of their licences. Thomas was also instrumental in acquiring the Watch House for St. Marylebone. He was minutely involved in the day-to-day business between the Lord of the manor (Harley) and the Vestry.

THE WATCH HOUSE

Professional policing in London did not begin until 1829 and before that vestries made whatever arrangements they could to apprehend criminals and have them tried by magistrates. Without proper street lighting the opportunities for crime were many and St Marylebone, just as in other parishes, appointed watchmen to suppress or avert as much as they were able, although the quality of watchmen was often lampooned.

Marylebone obtained an Act of Parliament to allow them to levy a Watch Rate, but had no Watch House to act as headquarters for the watchmen and in which to temporarily imprison any felons. Therefore, in 1733, the Vestry appealed to the Earl of Oxford via a petition prepared by William Thomas: "the parish …[is] infested with the idle and disorderly persons who frequently commit robberies and other disorders there…" As it happened, Harley had a manorial courthouse, built in 1729,[2] at the southern end of Marylebone Lane and it was this building which henceforth was used as the Watch House. It later became the centre for the

124. *Watchmen prepare for their night's work at the Watch House in Marylebone Lane. The man at the table is presumably signing them in. Aquatint by Rowlandson and Pugin c.1810.*

125.   The Watch House, now fronted by shops, in 1921. The Harley arms are over the door.

administration of St Marylebone and the Justices of the Peace met there as well.

We reproduce a photograph of the old Marylebone Watch House, which by then had become the premises of well-known booksellers Messrs J. and E. Bumpus Ltd which, in 1928, was also listed at 350 Oxford Street.

THE END OF THE OPEN VESTRY

In a way the 'open' vestry was as near democracy as was to be available but its replacement by a 'select' vestry in 1768 put the affluent in office for about 65 years. After all, in an open vestry meeting any householder could attend and make his voice and vote count, but sometimes meetings could become rowdy and too crowded and out of control. This hampered the efficient management of the parish.

The 3rd Duke of Portland – the Portlands were the new lords of the manor – was in favour of a select vestry. The system was that a Bill to Parliament was drawn up by leading (and therefore affluent) residents which would request the power to be a select vestry – the resulting Act would nominate a list of names for the first select vestry and those people themselves would appoint new ones as and when a death or a resignation would demand.

On 1 December 1767, the petition for a select

vestry (and an opposing petition) were presented and referred to a Parliamentary Committee. Notwithstanding that the petition opposing had more signatories and that the petition in favour was not well argued or supported, the Bill in favour of a select vestry was passed.

By 1768, Marylebone was an affluent town and its administration needed to reflect this. To be fair, most of the new vestrymen were owners of estates and businesses and their skills were suited to the administration of the parish in which they were resident. They were also accustomed to hard work. John Jones commenced as Clerk to the Paving Commissioners, but in 1770 he had become the Vestry Clerk. He remained Clerk to the Paving Commissioners, and also became Clerk to the Trustees of the Burial Ground, sealer of Weights and Measures and the supervising cockman at the workhouse; in 1781 he also became the Treasurer.

Jones spent his entire working life in the service of the Vestry. There are numerous examples of his 'unwearied diligence and assiduity' not least in the re-codifying of the Vestry Act and in opposition to a contentious Stratford Place Bill and in the reorganisation of the Watch. According to Sheppard, the whole administration of the parish came to depend on him.

At one point in Jones' career, he discovered that his own son-in-law, a tax collector, could not reconcile his records with the receipts. Jones himself made up the shortfall which he had by his persistence discovered, so unwilling was he that anyone connected with him should injure either his or the parish's reputation. By diligence and hard work the vestrymen and their appointees transformed the administration of St Marylebone.

In 1770, the maintenance of Oxford Street was taken over by the Vestry from the Turnpike Trust. The Vestry was more efficient, providing lighting, watchmen and repairs.

The select vestry eventually fell victim to the great reforming movements of the 19th century which were influenced by radical thinking derived from the American War of Independence and the French Revolution. As Sheppard points out, if Parliament was no longer willing to countenance the outrages of rotten boroughs, then how likely was Parliament to permit the continuance of governance of London by unelected officials?

The struggle between those agitating for elected representation on the Vestry and those opposing it in St. Marylebone began in 1827 and continued for five years. During that time Parliament too was very divided over the proposed Reform Bill which sought to get rid of many voting anomalies and to bring greater democracy. Marylebone's Select Vestry would have done well to heed the criticisms, but it did not, and the local tradesmen were not in a mood to compromise at the Vestry's secrecy and a number of insider transactions which, if not exactly corrupt, gave rise to dissatisfaction.

The new Whig government under Lord Grey gave a spur to reform and encouragement to London radicals. The vestrymen were asked to relinquish the principle of self-election and to support reform.

A Bill was introduced by John Cam Hobhouse in 1830 which would do away with undemocratic select vestries. A Select Committee interviewed a number of vestries, including Marylebone, and examined their procedures and administrations. It is interesting that William Crawford, a Marylebone parishioner, a Justice of the Peace, but not a vestryman, gave evidence relating to his own parish. He examined the parish accounts devised by John Jones and said to the Committee, 'With all the experience I have had in accounts, it cost me a great deal of labour before I could tell what they meant. They have none of the right principles of exhibiting accounts about them.' He went on, 'They were constructed on erroneous principles which defy human ingenuity to balance them in their present form'. One vestrymen was not ashamed to say that he had not 'time or talent to attend to the details of the business' and another said frankly that he had no liking for arithmetic – 'we never published more accounts than enough to satisfy our own curiosity'.[3]

The proposal before Parliament was that all ratepayers were to have one vote and every year one third of the vestrymen should retire and an equal number were to be elected in their place. There was to be an independent Board of Auditors elected on the same principle and voting was to be by ballot. The issue became not whether there would be elected vestrymen, but the qualifications of those who would do the electing: whether they would be only ratepayers or whether they would also have to be property owners.

Hobhouse's Act passed the Commons, got a rough reception in the Lords, but it finally received Royal Assent on October 1831 and the era of the select vestry was over. The last meeting of Marylebone's select vestry was on 21 April 1832.

The Reform Act of 1832 abolished rotten boroughs. After this the populous parishes of St Marylebone and St Pancras were made into one constituency. In the first subsequent parliamentary election there were a total of 21,630 electors: the successful candidates, E.B. Portman and Sir William Horne, secured 4,317 and 3,320 votes respectively. The Returning Officer reported:

> The exercise of the elective franchise for the first time, by the inhabitants of this populous Borough has been conducted with such harmony; that while it might have been expected that great excitement would have existed from the novelty of the proceedings, yet not a single breach of the peace occurred … reflecting the highest credit on the good taste, discernment and moderation, of the enlightened inhabitants of this important Borough.

Both the successful candidates had previously been MPs. Portman, a Whig, had represented a Dorset constituency consistently supporting Whig policies, while Horne had had a longer career in Parliament, having previously represented no fewer than three other constituencies. His political affiliations were less obvious but he was described as 'standing pledged to a vigilant and unremitting attention to the correction of all abuses'.

126. St Marylebone Town Hall, c. 1920.

MUNICIPAL BUILDINGS

On the south side of Marylebone Road, just west of Baker Street, are the former St Marylebone Town Hall and Central Library, both designed by Sir Edwin Cooper. The site of the town hall was purchased from Viscount Portman for £40,000 and the foundation stone was laid in 1914. However, the building was commandeered by the government during the First World War and it was not until 27 March 1920 that it was formally opened as a town hall.

Marylebone was the last of the London boroughs to adopt the Public Library Acts and it was not until 1923 that a temporary library was opened in the Town Hall. This was followed later by the handsome building next door.

The Library contains a collection of notable watercolours and drawings, though the local history section has now been removed to the Westminster City Archives.

LOCAL HOUSING

In the 20th century, the borough took on many projects to improve the amenities for the ordinary resident. By way of example only, social housing included the following residential estates: Crawford Place (1902), Fisherton Street (1927), Church Street (1950), Barrow Hill (1950), Townshend Estate (post war) Winchilsea House (1950) and a vast estate on Abbey Road/ Boundary Road (1953).

THE PUBLIC BATHS

A swimming pool and baths were opened in Seymour Place in 1874, designed by H. Saxon Snell. They were replaced by the present buildings, opened on 29 April 1937, and now called a Leisure Centre.

127. The swimming pool in the public baths in Seymour Place, opened in 1874. The architect was Saxon Snell.

BURYING THE DEAD

The old parish church in the High Street had a churchyard which, as the population of Marylebone increased dramatically, could not possibly cope with the increase in burials. In the 1730s the Vestry acquired from the Harleys some land south of Paddington Street, entered by today's Moxon Street, for a new burial ground. Marylebone's historian, Thomas Smith, in 1833 calculated that 80,000 people were buried there, a figure trumped by Edward Walford about forty years later when he thought that the figure was nearer 100,000. It is unsurprising that the Vestry had to find more space. In 1772 they bought some additional land from the Portmans on the north side of Paddington Street.

In the 19th century inner London burial grounds were gradually closed as either being too full or unhealthy. In 1885 the Paddington Street ground was converted to a public garden, officially opened by Princess Louise, a daughter of Queen Victoria, on 6 July 1886. Most of the tombs were removed (as they were all over London) but the Fitzpatrick Mausoleum was left because of its design. The Mausoleum is of Portland stone, with an ogee dome. It was erected by the Hon. Richard Fitzpatrick to the memory of his beloved wife the Hon Susanna Fitzpatrick, who died 28 March 1759 aged 30.

Many metropolitan parishes had to find land outside their own boundaries for burials. St Marylebone opened a cemetery at East End Road in East Finchley in 1854, then 'a retired and rural spot' of farmland. Famous names buried there include Quintin Hogg, founder of the Regent Street Polytechnic, painter George Hayter, Thomas Huxley, Leopold Stokowski, and a member of the Crazy Gang, Jimmy Nervo.

The Garden at the top of Marylebone High Street marks the site of the old parish church and its churchyard, built in 1400, rebuilt 1741 and demolished in 1949. The actual foundations of the church are noted on a plaque in the Garden. This historic ground was designed as a garden-

128. The public garden on the site of the old churchyard in Marylebone High Street.

of-rest in 1951 to celebrate the Festival of Britain.

The churchyard was the burial site of many notable people including

James Figg (d. 1734) pugilist *(see p. 122)*;

Edward Forset, (sometimes Forsett) (1553-1630), Lord of the manor, a political writer (including on the concept of the divine right of kings) and playwright, and was involved in the prosecutions after the Gunpowder Plot of 1605;

James Gibbs (1682-1754) one of Britain's most influential architects, designer of St. Peter's in Vere Street and the Oxford Market, and of the Cavendish Square development. Gibbs also designed St. Mary-le-Strand and St. Martin-in-the-Fields;

Edmond Hoyle (1672-1769) a writer known for his detailed descriptions of whist, backgammon, chess, quadrille, piquet and brag.

The *3rd Duke of Portland (William Henry Cavendish-Bentinck),* (1738-1809), Lord of the manor;

Allan Ramsay (1713-1784), who painted many portraits of the Hanoverian monarchy, even managing to make Queen Charlotte positively handsome. He also painted tender portraits of his wife and children and other less well-known personages. His most striking portrait is a full length depiction of the handsome and charismatic 3rd Marquess of Bute. He lived at what is now numbered 24 Harley Street;

John Rysbrack (1694-1770) the Flemish sculptor who came to London in 1720 and sculpted among others Isaac Newton, Bolingbroke and Horace Walpole;

George Stubbs (1724 -1806) painter, especially of horses and dogs. In 1763 he bought a house at 24 Somerset Street, Portman Square where he lived until his death;

Charles Wesley (1707-1788) a leader of the Methodist movement and younger brother of John Wesley, chiefly remembered for the many hymns he composed.

[1] This is a classic work on the administration of a London local authority. This chapter has relied heavily on its information.

[2] Illustration 124 shows the interior of the old watch house. The most famous detainee was James Boswell, biographer of Dr Johnson, who was arrested one night in 1790 for crying out the hour in the street, which was strictly the prerogative of the Watch.

[3] F.H.W. Sheppard, *Local Government in St Marylebone 1688-1835* (1958), 290.

Artisans, Artists and Writers

The Royal Academy was founded in 1768. This, and the development of the Portland Estate and the later Portman Estate, encouraged artists and skilled craftsmen to live near their potential clients in Marylebone. As Ann Saunders (née Cox Johnson) points out in the introduction to her directory *Handlist of Painters, Sculptors & Architects associated with St Marylebone 1760-1960*,

> "For the artist who lived there [Marylebone] patrons were within walking distance, there was space for workshops, light and clear air for studios and farmlands for pleasant exercise, stretching unbroken to the heights of Hampstead and Highgate"

SKILLED CRAFTSMEN OF THE GEORGIAN PERIOD IN MARYLEBONE

The opulent residential building in Marylebone between 1700 and 1820 required highly skilled plasterers, stuccoists, workers in scagliola, joiners and carpenters, among others. Very often several skills were embodied in the same artisan. Geoffrey Beard in his work, *Craftsmen and Interior Decoration in England 1660 to 1820*, provides a directory of some of these craftsmen with notes of the places in London (and outside London) where they worked. Some had professional association with a titled family outside London who then hired their services when the family built their house in town. Architects such as the Adam brothers, James Gibbs and John Nash assembled a group of craftsmen who worked to their standards and styles. The Rose firm of plasterers is an example: their projects in London were numerous.

Transport being what it was, the artisans lived locally within a mile or two of the current project. A few are of French or Italian origin.

Below, is a small sampling of these men, to show the variety of those who either worked on notable buildings in Marylebone or nearby, or who lived there.

Joseph Alcott (1786-1815), carpenter and scagliola[1] worker, lived at 81 Queen Anne Street in 1795 and worked on houses in Piccadilly and at Goodwood.

Oliver Alken (d. 1769), carver, lived in Little Titchfield Street. On his death he entrusted his son and daughter to another master carver James Thorne of Westminster and Richard Lawrence.

Giuseppe Artari (late 17th century-1769). There were three Artaris, and their history is complex, but they were all stuccoists. Giuseppe worked extensively with James Gibbs, in 1723-4 on St. Peter's, Vere Street and in 1729 in Cavendish Square, as well as many places outside London and on the continent.

James Boyle (*fl.* 1763), carver and gilder, was at the Golden Eagle in Great Pulteney Street and he carved in the Italian, French, Gothic and Chinese tastes.

Joseph Brown (*fl.* 1814-1820) scagliola and marble worker, worked for John Nash from Nash's premises in Carmarthen Street.

Clement Cryer (*fl.* 1769-1800) worked on commissions for Rose, whose premises were in Queen Anne Street East.[2] (*See below re Joseph Rose, plasterer*)

John Cuneot (*fl.* 1744-62) a carver and son of a French carver, he worked for the Duke of Montagu and is best known for his work for the Duke of Northumberland. He lived nearby in Warwick Street, Golden Square.

John Howgill (*fl.* 1727), a carver who did work on Lord Bingley's house[3] in Cavendish Square.

George Jackson (1756-1840), plasterer. The firm George Jackson & Sons Ltd. (at 49 Rathbone Place) published a history of the company which records 'When Robert Adam bought the famous recipe for composition from John Liardet, George Jackson made reverse moulds in boxwood and pressed out the ornament in this material'. The firm also introduced 'fibrous plaster'.

Isaac Mansfield (*fl.* 1697-1739) plasterer, lived in Henrietta Place a few doors from James Gibbs and did work for James Brydges, the 1st Duke of Chandos.

Richard Norris (*fl.* 1756-75), coppersmith and brazier, lived in Jermyn Street and worked on 20

129.   *The carton-Pierre ornament factory of George Jackson in Rathbone Place, 1908.*

Portman Square, Home House in 1775.

Joseph Rose Jr. (1745-1799), plasterer; with his father, brother and uncle who were all plasterers, they formed the firm of Joseph Rose & Co. which monopolised the important plasterwork of the Adam period. It appears that he was married in 1717 at Marylebone Church. The family had their premises at Queen Anne Street East and they worked in Marylebone in Chandos Street, Grafton Street, Mansfield Street, Portland Place (at both Nos. 16 and 4) and at 20 Portman Square, Home House.

ARCHITECTS, ARTISTS, ENGRAVERS AND SCULPTORS

The architects, painters, engravers, sculptors were so numerous in Marylebone in this period of its greatest development that we can give only a small selection of the best known names.

John Constable (1776-1837) was at 85 Charlotte Street and also 50 Rathbone Place very near the plasterers George Jackson & Co. mentioned above.

Richard Cosway lived in Berkeley Street, then Pall Mall and then on the east corner of Stratford Place and Oxford Street. Cosway and his wife Maria were 'style setters' who educated and entertained their clients and patrons. His portraits on ivory include not only that of the Prince of Wales, but many titled persons in London society. Cosway also did a portrait of Mie Mie the wife of the 3rd Marquess of Hertford and grandmother of Richard Wallace after whom the Wallace Collection is named.

J. G. Crace & Son at 38 Wigmore Street[4] were one of the most important decorating firms of the 18th and 19th centuries, responsible for many of the decorative schemes of the Prince Regent including that at the Brighton Pavilion

Eugene Delcroix (1799-1863), the famous French painter, lived at 8 Somerset Street, a street which no longer exists off Portman Square.

Sir Charles Eastlake (1793-1865), head of the National Gallery and an influential figure in English decoration was at 29 Devonshire Street in 1830.

Henry Fuseli (1741–1825), originally Swiss,

130. *John Constable.*

he lived at what became 72 Queen Anne Street and then moved on to 13 Berners Street from 1804 to 1825.

James Gibbs, (1682-1754), architect, the employer of so many of the skilled craftsmen named above, was at 9, 10 and 11 Henrietta Street.

Sir George Hayter (1792-1871), had a number of Marylebone addresses, including Margaret Street, Wells Street, Wimpole Street and Stratford Place.

Sir Edwin Landseer (1802-1873), Queen Victoria's favourite artist and the painter of so many portraits of animals, including Prince Albert's greyhound, was at 33 Foley Street 1815-23 and then moved on to 1 St. John's Wood Road.

John Linnell (1792-1882) was at 11 Queen Street (now Harrowby Street) and then at 35 Rathbone Place.

The sculptor **Joseph Nollekens** (1737-1823) has a plaque recording his residence at 44 Mortimer Street. He also worked for Joseph Rose Jnr, the plasterer (*see above*).

131. Sir John Soane, from the painting by Thomas Lawrence.

John Opie (1761-1807), painter, was at 8 Berners Street from 1791 until his death.

Sir Henry Raeburn (1756-1823), portraitist, was at 1 Hinde Street by 1802.

Allan Ramsay (1713-1784) was at 24 Harley Street (formerly No. 67). He was court painter to George III and his portraits, while flattering, are of the most subtle and alluring quality.

George Romney (1734-1802), portraitist, was at 24 Cavendish Square, later at No. 32.

John Charles Felix Rossi (1762-1839), a sculptor, rented a workshop in Marylebone Park from 1798 until 1810.

Sir John Soane, (1753-1837) architect and collector, who designed Holy Trinity church on Marylebone Road, lived in Cavendish Street, and then from 1782-86 at 33 Margaret Street and afterwards in Welbeck Street. Later, of course, he lived in Lincoln's Inn Fields, where his house is now the Soane Museum.

George Stubbs (1724-1806), famous for his paintings of horses and dogs, lived from 1764 to his death in 1806 at 24 Somerset Street, a street now beneath the northern extension of Selfridge's.

Sir John Tenniel (1820-1914), creator of the drawings in *Alice in Wonderland* and *The Owl and the Pussy Cat,* was at 22 Gloucester Place from 1837 to 1843.

The landscape artist, **J.M.W. Turner** (1775-1851) was at 35 Harley Street (formerly 64); the plaque to him is over the door of 23 Queen Anne Street on the front of the office of the Howard de Walden Estate.

Benjamin West (1738-1820), artist, sent paintings into the Royal Academy from 14 Newman Street, 1775-1820.

EIGHTEENTH-CENTURY WRITERS

Soon after **Samuel Johnson** (1709-1784) came to London from Lichfield, he and his wife took lodgings in what is now Eastcastle Street – in the 1730s this bordered countryside. Initially, Johnson worked as a journalist. In 1742, he began cataloguing the 40,000 volume library of Edward Harley, 2nd Earl of Oxford, who was also the Estate owner and developer of Cavendish Square. By the 1760s, Johnson (having moved away) returned to Marylebone to visit friends, particularly the painter Allan Ramsay. Johnson's great friend and biographer, James Boswell (1740-95), spent the last five years of his life in Marylebone at 122 Great Portland Street .

Edward Gibbon (1737-94) lived at 7 Bentinck Street between 1773 and 1783 when he wrote part of his monumental work, *The History of the Decline and Fall of the Roman Empire.* In 1774 Gibbon was elected as a member of 'The Club' which Johnson founded in 1764 with Joshua Reynolds and whose members included Edmund Burke, Oliver Goldsmith, the actor David Garrick, and Charles James Fox.

When the Irish poet, **Tom Moore** (1779-1852) came to London at the age of twenty to study law and lodged at 85 George Street, it was then at the lower end of the market, populated by the impoverished French.[5] Moore was handsome, witty and for a while a social darling. When a book of his poetry received unfavourable notice in the *Edinburgh Review,* he challenged Francis Jeffrey, the reviewer, to a duel at Chalk Farm Fields. Moore provided the pistols but they were both arrested and it was revealed that the pistols were loaded with paper pellets. Byron devoted a verse on the affair in *English Bards and Scottish Reviewers*:

Can none remember that eventful day,
That ever glorious, almost fatal fray,
When Little's leadless pistols met his eye,
And Bow Street myrmidons stood laughing by?

Moore spent little time in London after this event.

NINETEENTH-CENTURY WRITERS

Charles Dickens (1812-1870) and his family moved into No. 1 Devonshire Terrace in 1839 opposite the York Gate entrance to Regent's Park, on the site of 15-17 Marylebone Road. It was his home for the next eleven years. He commented that the house was one 'of great promise (and great premium), undeniable situation and excessive splendour ... I am in ecstatic restlessness.'

In his biography of Dickens, John Forster described the house as a

'handsome structure with a spacious brick-walled garden between it and the New [Marylebone] Road. The entrance set back a little from the street, and an impressive portico of brick and stone, and curving into the garden were two semicircular bow windows ... Within, a large vestibule opened on a spacious square hall and a stairway curving up to the left, a library on the right with steps descending into the garden, and behind these, splendid with ornamental columns, a dining room that also overlooked the garden and the coach house in the rear. On the floors above were a drawing room and bedrooms and nursery.'

The nursery proved an asset as five children were born here and the 'excessive splendour' managed to accommodate his wife, sister-in-law, four maids and a man-servant. Nearby Regent's Park was ideally situated for the nurses to take the children for walks and fresh air. However Dickens expressed concern about the rowdy elements frequenting the Park particularly the bad language they used, 'I found this evil to be so abhorrent there, that I called public attention to it.' Dickens insisted that the police take a

seventeen-year-old girl into custody for using 'such language in the streets'.

While living here, Dickens wrote *The Old Curiosity Shop, Dombey and Son, Martin Chuzzlewit, Barnaby Rudge, A Christmas Carol* and *David Copperfield*. Some of the characters from these novels are depicted in a bas-relief panel erected in 1960 outside the office block at 15 Marylebone Road.

Marylebone also provided settings in *Dombey and Son* (1848). Mr Dombey's house is described as large

'on the shady side of a tall, dark, dreadfully genteel street in the region between Portland Place and Bryanston Square. It was a corner house with great wide areas containing cellars frowned upon by barred windows, and leered at by crooked-eyed doors leading to dustbins. It was a house of dismal state...'

Dickens lived near St. Marylebone Church and had his son baptised there. The ceremony is described in *Dombey and Son*: 'Presently the clerk ... came up with a jug of warm water, and said something, as he poured it into the font, about taking the chill off; which millions of gallons boiling hot could not have done for the occasion.' Many of the characters in *David Copperfield*, it has been suggested, were based on well-known persons then living in Marylebone.

Wilkie Collins (1824-1889) was both a fellow writer and friend of Dickens. Collins was a Marylebone resident for most of his life, living at 38 Blandford Square, 13 Hanover Terrace, 12 Cavendish Square, 65 Gloucester Place and died at 82 Wimpole Street. Dickens and Collins took holidays and dined together for a period of five years, and Dickens employed him to write for *Household Words* and *All the Year Round*. In 1860, Collins lived with Caroline Graves at 12 Harley Street at a time when his literary career became more successful.

After breaking with the publishers of *Household Words*, Dickens founded a weekly journal intended to appeal to all classes of readers, *All The Year Round*. It began in 1859 with the serialisation of Dickens' *A Tale of Two Cities*. The second serialisation was Collins' most famous work, *The Woman in White*, which became an enormous success and was a turning point in his career.

Not only did Collins live with Caroline Graves, but during the mid-1860s met and also lived with Martha Rudd with whom he had three children. He divided his time between the two households until his death in September 1889. His opium addiction as well as his relationships with the two women led to estrangement from Dickens who knew the details of Collins's private life, just as Collins knew about Dickens's affair with the young actress Ellen Ternan. Dickens, commenting to a friend in 1861, about Collins' domestic arrangements wrote,

'He has made his rooms in Harley Street very handsome and comfortable. We never speak of the (female) skeleton in that house and I therefore have not the least idea of the state of his mind on that subject. I hope it does not run in any matrimonial groove. I cannot imagine any good coming of such an end in this instance.'

Collins wrote many of his twenty-two novels under the influence of laudanum, whose use, in various proprietary formulas, was both widespread and unregulated in the 19th century.

Elizabeth Barrett (1806-1861) an invalid much under the patriarchal rule of Barrett senior, moved with her family to a house on the site of number 50 Wimpole Street in 1838. In 1845, with her career established, she began exchanging letters with Robert Browning (1812-1889). The following year, defying her father's refusal to sanction the marriage, Elizabeth and Robert married at St Marylebone Church. From the ceremony, she returned home but a week later, left for Italy with Robert in the hope that the warmer climate would help her recover her health. They rarely returned to England. In 1861 she died from the complications of a severe cold.

The story, well known, was the subject of a film in 1934 starring Charles Laughton and Norma Shearer, *The Barretts of Wimpole Street*. This focuses on how Elizabeth and her younger sister Henrietta, with help from their many siblings, conspire to defy the strictures of their tyrannical father.

132. Elizabeth Barrett (Browning), from a drawing by Field Talfourd.

Anthony Trollope (1815-1882) lived at 39 Montagu Square in 1873 for eight years, where he worked to a rigorous and regular schedule, assisted by his niece, Florence Bland, as secretary. During his time there he wrote, *The Eustace Diamonds* (1873), *Phineas Redux* (1874), *The Prime Minister* (1876), *The American Senator* and *Is he the Popenjoy?* (1878). By 1880 advancing age brought asthma and in July, for the benefit of better air, Trollope moved to Harting Grange, near Petersfield, Hampshire. Returning to London he died at 34 Welbeck Street on 6 December 1882.

William Makepeace Thackeray (1811-1863) used Marylebone Gardens as a setting in *Catherine* (1839), 'There was given, at Marylebone Gardens, a grand concert and entertainment', and Regent's Park is referred to in *The Bedford Row Conspiracy* (1840) and in *Vanity Fair* (1847). The Park was also a source for **Virginia Woolf** in *Mrs. Dalloway* (1925). In Woolf's diaries she records how she found both solace and inspiration there: 'There is no doubt that the greatest happiness in the world is walking through Regent's Park on a green ... wet ... red pink and blue evening.'

TWENTIETH-CENTURY WRITERS

John Buchan (1875-1940) lived at 76 Portland Place between 1913 and 1919. While ill in bed in 1914, he wrote his most famous novel, *The Thirty-Nine Steps*. He refers to Marylebone in his books, *The Power House* (1916), *The Path of The King* (1921) and *Mr Standfast* (1919).

H.G. Wells (1866-1946) lived at 13 Hanover Terrace in 1937 until his death in 1946. He refers to Marylebone in *Under the Knife* (1896) and *The Invisible Man* (1897): 'After a successful experiment on a neighbour's cat, Griffin has walked from his lodgings near Great Portland Street to meditate on his next steps.' In *War of the Worlds* (1898) during the Martian invasion of England, Wells describes the panic in parts of London:

'There were one or two cartloads of refugees passing along Oxford Street, and several in the Marylebone Road, but so slowly was the news spreading that Regent Street and Portland Place were full of their usual Sunday-night promenaders ... As I emerged from the top of Baker Street, I saw far away over the trees in the clearness of the sunset the hood of the Martian giant from which the howling proceeded.'

Edgar Wallace (1875-1932), the prolific crime writer who wrote over 175 novels, lived at Clarence Gate Gardens near Regent's Park and in 1928-9 at 31 Portland Place. He refers to the latter street in *The Green Rust* (1919), and to Marylebone Road in *The Clue of the Twisted Candle* (1932).

The poet, critic and dramatist, **T.S. Eliot** (1888-1965), originally from Missouri, lived at No. 18, Crawford Mansions in Crawford Street. He came to Britain in 1915, lodging in what was then a rough part of London. He struggled at first for recognition, finding employment at a bank. The *Waste Land* was published in 1922 and he became a British subject in 1927. Eliot produced a substantial body of poetry, drama and literary

criticism and was awarded the Nobel Prize for Literature in 1948. By then, he had long departed Crawford Street. Eliot , while an editor at Faber & Faber, rejected the manuscript of *Animal Farm*, Orwell's prescient parable on the workings of communism. Eliot also lived in an apartment at 9 Clarence Gate Gardens between 1920 and 1930.

[1] Scagliola from the Italian 'chips': a crushed alabaster and plaster mix with pigment made to mimic marble, stone and other semi precious stones, including porphyry. Requires great technical skill; now valued for its historic interest and beauty.

[2] Now Queen Anne Street.

[3] Lord Bingley had been one of the early lessees of the Harleys in Cavendish Square, having built a house on the west side of the Square. He died in 1731.

[4] The premises had a distinct bow-fronted window in Wigmore Street.

[5] Gordon Mackenzie, *Marylebone, Great City North of Oxford Street* (1972), 242.

Further Reading

Adburgham, Alison, *Shopping in Style (1979)*

Ashbridge, Arthur, *St Marylebone and its Anglo-Saxon Manors* (1918)

Ashford, E, Bright, *Lisson Green: a Domesday village in St. Marylebone* (1960, St. Marylebone Society).

Ashford, E. Bright, *Tyburn Village and Stratford Place* (1969 St Marylebone Society)

Bailey, Nick, *Fitzrovia* (1981)

Barber, Peter and Jacomelli, Peter, *Continental Taste: Ticinese emigrants and their Café-Restaurants in Britain 1847-1987* (1997 Camden History Society)

Beard, Geoffrey, *Craftsmen and Interior Decoration in England 1660-1820* (1981)

Black, Gerry, *Living up West: Jewish Life in London's West End* (1994)

Black, Gerry, *Jewish London, an illustrated history* (2003)

Black, N. *Walking London's Medical History* (2006 The Royal Society of Medicine Press Ltd).

Brooke, Alan & Brandon, David, *Tyburn, London's Fatal Tree* (2004).

Brown, Ian R. A., *The Langham* (2005, Langham Hotels)

Byrne, Andrew, *London's Georgian Houses* (1986)

Chancellor, E. Beresford, *Wanderings in Marylebone: a gossip about squares and the streets* (1926)

Chancellor, E. Beresford, *The 18th Century in London* (1920)

Cherry, Bridget & Pevsner, Nikolaus, *Buildings of England. London 3: North West* (1991)

Clayton, Antony, *Subterranean City: Beneath the streets of London* (2000)

Corina, Maurice, *Fine Silks & Oak Counters: Debenhams 1778-1978* (1978)

Cox-Johnson, Ann *see* Saunders, Ann

Davis, Dorothy, *A History of Shopping* (1966)

Flemming, Percy, *Harley Street from early times to the present day* (1939)

Harley, Ian, *St Marylebone Charity School* (2000)

Honeycombe, Gordon, *Selfridges* (1984)

Hughes, Peter, *The Founders of the Wallace Collection* (2006)

McDonald, Erica and Smith, David J, *Pineapples and Pantomimes: A history of Church Street and Lisson Green* (1992)

Mackenzie, G., *Marylebone: great city north of Oxford Street* (1972)

McNeal, E.G.B., *St Marylebone Grammar School, A brief history till 1954* (1979)

McNeal, E.G.B., *St Marylebone Grammar School: A view of Events 1954-1981* (1981)

Macpherson, Hugh (ed), *John Spedan Lewis 1885-1963* (1985)

Mallett, Donald, *The Greatest Collector: Lord Hertford and the Founding of the Wallace Collection* (1979).

Marylebone Journal

Matthews, H. J. *History of St. Marylebone (1960).*

Morley, Malcolm, *The Old Marylebone Theatre* (1960 St. Marylebone Society)

Morley, Malcolm, *Royal West London Theatre* (1962 St Marylebone Society)

Neate, Alan R. *The St. Marylebone Workhouse and Institution 1730-1965* (2003 rev. edn by St Marylebone Society, City of Westminster Archives and the University of Westminster)

Pentelowe, Mike and Rowe, Marsha, *Characters of Fitzrovia* (2001)

Porter, Roy, *London: A Social History* (1995).

Saunders, Ann (née Cox-Johnson), *Handlist of Painters, Sculptors and Architects associated with St Marylebone 1760-1960* (1963)

Saunders, Ann, *Regent's Park from 1086 to the present* (1981 rev. edn. Bedford College)

Saunders, Ann, *The Art and Architecture of London* (1984)

Service, Alastair, *London 1900* (1979)

Sheppard, F. H. W., *Local government in St. Marylebone, 1688-1835* (1958)

Smith, T, *A topographical and historical account of the parish of St. Mary-le-Bone* (1833).

Summerson, John, *Georgian London* (rev. edn 1988)

Tallis, John, *London Street Views 1838-40* (1969 Facsimile edition London Topographical Society)

Thorold, P. *The London Rich* (1999).

Webster, A. D., *The Regent's Park and Primrose Hill* (1911)

Weinreb, Ben & Hibbert, Christopher, *The London Encyclopaedia* (1983).

Westminster History Review, Nos. 3 and 5 (2005 and 2007 City of Westminster Archives)

Whipham, Thomas, *Montagu Square* (1990)

White, J. *London in the Nineteenth Century* (2007).

Whitehead, Jack, *The Growth of St Marylebone and Paddington* (rev. edn.1990)

Wise, Dorothy (ed) *Diary of William Tayler, Footman 1837* (1998 City of Westminster Archives with the St. Marylebone Society).

Wood, Ethel M., *The Polytechnic and its Founder Quintin Hogg* (1932)

INDEX

*An asterisk denotes an
illustration or caption*